Understanding Everyday Experience
Series Editor: Laurie Taylor

ANN SHEARER

Disability:
Whose
Handicap?

BASIL BLACKWELL · OXFORD

© Ann Shearer 1981

First published 1981
Basil Blackwell Publisher Ltd
108 Cowley Road
Oxford OX4 1JF
England

British Library Cataloguing in Publication Data

Shearer, Ann
    Disability. – (Understanding everyday experience)
    1. Handicapped
    I. Title   II. Series
    362.4 HV 1568

    ISBN 0-631-12671-6
    ISBN 0-631-12768-2 Pbk

Typeset by Cambrian Typesetters,
Farnborough, Hants
Printed in Great Britain by Billing & Sons Ltd
Guildford, London, Oxford, Worcester.

Contents

Acknowledgements

This book would not have been possible without the help of the hundred and more people who responded to my request for personal views of living with a disability. They remain anonymous; where there are names against previously unpublished material in the text, these are pseudonyms. But I hope the reality of personal experience comes through. My thanks to all the people who shared it so generously. I'd also like to thank friends and colleagues in the Campaign for Mentally Handicapped People, l'Arche and the Disability Alliance, from whom I've learned a great deal over the years. Rosemary and Gunnar Dybwad, Micheline Mason, Mike and Judith Oliver, Ann Thwaite and Rosalie Wilkins know why they get a special mention. My thanks to them all, and to John Davey and Laurie Taylor. None of them, of course, carries any responsibility for anything I say here: that's mine.

A.S.

Preface

A recent television programme attempted to dramatize the experience of disability by placing one of its reporters in a wheelchair and sending him off to make his way around town. The resulting frustrations were quite enough to make the point about the token way in which we cater for a large section of the disabled. Special lavatories for the disabled were sited within restaurants whose entrance arrangements virtually excluded the possibility of the disabled ever actually arriving at their tables let alone using the toilet facilities. Specially constructed ramps led the way into pedestrian precincts from which there was no effective exit.

Such practical demonstrations are useful reminders of the half-hearted manner in which we attempt to accommodate the disabled amongst us. But they tell very little of the full story. As long as disablement means little more than the difficulties of getting around in a wheelchair, then the solutions are simple. Just a few physical corrections to the environment will get rid of most of the frustrations and discomforts experienced by those who are less than one hundred per cent able.

The great merit of Ann Shearer's book is that it refuses to accept disablement as something which is limited to such a special group of people. As she remarks, 'Each and every one of us knows moments of inability, moments when the body and mind that we take for granted let us down, refuse to work for us.' The line between this and finding ourselves categorized as disabled is only one of degree, a matter which is as dependent upon the demands which society makes upon us as the intrinsic quality of our inability. This, as Ann Shearer forcibly argues, makes the real question not how we can help disabled people in their adjustment to society, but 'how far is society willing to adjust its patterns and expectations to include its members who have disabilities, and to remove the handicaps that are now imposed on their inevitable limitations'.

Neither will Ann Shearer allow that the discussion of the disabled should be confined to simple questions of their physical mobility. She relentlessly pursues in the areas of housing, education, work, and politics, the ways in which present practises place unnecessary extra burdens upon the disabled — the ways in which a disability is converted into a handicap.

This is a brave campaigning book which goes to the heart of many of our current hypocrisies. Its author is not arguing that we should be concerned about what she has to say because someday the majority of us will become partially disabled (which we will) but because our readiness to alleviate some of the current handicaps says something about 'our understanding of the essential thread of experience that binds us all into a common humanity'. To reject that common experience is to reject a part of ourselves. 'If we accept it, we could all find ourselves a little nearer wholeness'.

Laurie Taylor

1

Starting Points

There was nothing that particularly distinguished the girl from the others around her. A bit on the plump side, perhaps — but in that out-of-school stream there were others fatter, others thinner. The staff would say that she shone academically, but that is not a quality that you'd recognize at first glance. It was on the games field, in the gym, at the swimming-baths, that she stood out. There, she was the one whose body seemed to stop working for her, the one who trailed ungainly behind the ball, flopped across the vaulting-horse, stood shivering at the side of the pool. She knew that if she ran up the games field she would start to wheeze, that the vaulting-horse was waiting to swell to catch her, the water waiting to close over her head. It all looked so easy when the others did it. They would never understand that what was normal for them was impossible for her.

There was nothing particular to distinguish the boy from the others, either, unless it was a certain ease in his body, or the sort of high spirits that are infectious. Yet in the mathematics lesson, he was transformed. His whole personality seemed crushed by that piece of paper in front of him. Asked to explain the problem, his usual articulateness deserted him. He stammered, he scowled, he failed dismally to make sense of the activities of ten men pouring pints of water into a bath from which an eleventh had pulled the plug. What he hated worse than his own incomprehension was the fact that everyone else seemed to find the problem perfectly soluble, even enjoyable.

Each and every one of us knows moments of inability, moments when the body and mind that we take for granted

1

let us down, refuse to work for us. Each and every one of us has felt frustration at physical and mental limitations, and perhaps something nearer despair as we sense an isolation and rejection from a world that others seem to enjoy so easily. Not many of us have survived adolescence without sometimes being overwhelmed at our own apparant abnormality, at the lack of 'fit' between ourselves and the demands of the world that everyone else seems to be taking in their stride.

As life goes on, these moments probably get fewer. The inabilities no longer overwhelm us, for we find that the world will accept that we have abilities as well. We learn to avoid the places and situations that show up the first and find our way into those where we can use the second. Occasionally, the old feelings will come up and catch us unawares and undefended. A broken toe will throw us off balance and turn our environment into a place to be negotiated with care; a heavy cold will throw cotton wool between us and our thoughts, turn other people's conversation into a gabble that goes too fast. The girl, now a woman, still knows her moments of physical panic, still has her stabs of the isolation of the games field. But she also knows that her legs will carry her well enough for everyday purposes. The boy, now a man, can still feel something of his old resentment and helplessness when his employer questions one of his decisions, can sometimes still feel ill-equipped to cope with the demands of the computer age. But he also knows that for the purposes of balancing his bank account, his maths is good enough. They have both learned, as we all do, that the world is made up of people with a whole range of physical and mental strengths and weaknesses, and they have found that they fit in pretty well. And if, as they get older, they feel more of the weaknesses and fewer of the strengths, well, that's normal enough.

The mix of abilities and inabilities that goes to make up the human race is a broad one. The woman's physical abilities are as far from those of the Olympic athlete as they are from those of the woman who, because of an accident of birth, can't walk at all and must go about in a wheelchair. The man's understanding is as far from that of a Nobel prize-winning physicist as it is from that of the man who can only use the

2

shops by proferring a handful of money and seeing what he gets back. The woman who can't walk is, as it happens, a gifted mathematician. The man who can't count is a competent swimmer. Both of them have their quota of other gifts as well. But somehow, they are no longer seen as able in some situations and un-able in others. Instead, a blanket description is thrown over them. They are 'disabled'.

Immediately, the perception changes. The continuum of ability and inability is broken, a new vocabulary comes into play. We do not talk about people who are overweight as 'the fats', or people who are short-sighted as 'the myopics', because fatness or myopia is only one of their attributes, not anywhere near a complete description of the people. Yet people who have cerebral palsy become 'the spastics', people who are mentally retarded 'the subnormals', people who have arthritis 'the arthritics'. By turning a description of a condition into a description of people, we are saying that this is all we really need to know about them. We confirm their 'abnormality'.

They are different enough, these people, to have their own UN Declaration of Rights over and above the one to which we all, as human beings, refer. 'The term "disabled person" ', it says, 'means any person unable to ensure by himself or herself wholly or partly the necessities of a normal individual and/or social life, as the result of a deficiency, either congenital or not, in his or her physical or mental capabilities.' Yet which of us can, whatever our abilities? In our complex societies, we are all dependent on a whole host of others to sustain our everyday life.

They pose problems enough to our administrators, these people, to attract a whole host of special bureaucratic arrangements, over and above those available to all citizens. So both Denmark and Sweden, for instance, have, in post-war years, had central boards within their welfare bureaucracy to deal specifically with services to people who are mentally retarded. So there are now special bureaux and offices within Federal government departments in the USA to deal with services to people with a variety of disabilities, and special agencies like the President's Committee on Mental Retardation or the President's Committee on Employment of the Handicapped as

3

well. So in Britain, there is a special Minister for the Disabled.

Yet the agencies themselves have no precisely quantified and defined clientele. The existence of those agencies doesn't bring us nearer to a categoric definition of the people we call 'disabled'. In Britain, for example, we can take the official survey and come up with the estimate that three millions of us, or nearly eight per cent of the population, have some physical impairment. We learn that nearly three per cent of the population is 'handicapped' by this in its ability to perform a small number of self-care tasks. We can take Townsend's findings, based on a broader definition of essential tasks and including people with some degree of mental retardation, and double the figures.[1] Yet, important though such definitions are, to the planning and delivery of welfare services, they don't define the people. Would the inability to run to catch a bus, to go up and down stairs, reach an overhead shelf or understand a variety of everyday actions still make a person 'handicapped' if the buses waited for their passengers, ramps replaced the stairs, shelves were set at waist level, or teachers were more skilled?

The needs of the 'disabled' population are seen as different enough from those of the majority for them to use a whole range of special welfare services and provisions. We see them in special schools, in special workplaces, in special residential institutions. But if they left those places, would they still be defined as so 'different', so 'abnormal'? They also, after all, have their individual place on the continuum of ability and inability that makes up human society.

Why the cut-off? The difference between the people called 'disabled' and the majority is simply that they have less room for manoeuvre as they make their way about their society. Most people can conceal their inabilities most of the time, or avoid getting into situations where these will become apparent. People who have severe disabilities cannot, because their inabilities are in areas that are considered indispensable to coping with 'normal' life and because the world is organized around an assumption that everyone has a range of fundamental abilities. It is a short step from that assumption to the perception of people with disabilities as being fundamentally

4

different. It is a short step again to the provision of services and patterns of life which confirm that difference.

Yet the experiences of disability in this book say something else. They touch each one of us, in however fleeting and muted a form. They say that, underpinning all the obvious differences in ability, all the varieties of situation in which people find themselves, there is a common thread of experience. They say that the difference between what people defined as 'disabled' live with every day and the everyday experience of us all is not one of kind, but only one of degree.

This is not to take refuge in a philosophy that says that because everyone is disabled, then no one is. Much of the book is given over to looking at ways in which society responds to the reality of disability. It is not to underestimate the frustrations, difficulties and problems that disability may bring. 'I imagine', says one woman:

> that everyone in the world has felt the frustration of not understanding a problem, or not being able to reach a ripe blackberry, or not having enough money to buy a desired object. Being disabled is having such denials all day, every day and forever. Nothing, but nothing, makes the disability less restricting than to end the disability. If this is impossible, one has to learn to live with a limitation or drawback as surely as greasy hair, bad skin or an ugly face have to be accepted as part of life.[2]

It doesn't take much thought to recognize that living with greasy hair presents fewer problems than living, as this woman does, with her severe physical limitations.

Yet her experience finds its echoes in the experience of all of us, simply because we are all human and so all a mixture of strength and weakness, light and dark, fit and misfit. The point seems almost too obvious to make. We acknowledge it in our everyday vocabulary: we talk of being 'crippled' with indecision, 'paralysed' by shyness, 'blinded' by ambition. Yet people with disabilities find themselves having to underline the point over and over again. 'What does the disabled person face every day?' asks one woman:

Frustration, dependency, indignity and often pain and suffering. The able-bodied suffer all these at some time, but never all at once and every day, without end. And what special equipment have the disabled got? None. They are the same jumble of vices and virtues, the same jumble of needs. And this is the point, isn't it? Our bodies may not look nice or function properly, but our minds, hearts and emotions are the same.

The recognition may be an uncomfortable one. It makes us all look rather differently at the people defined as 'separate', perhaps question the ways in which the definition is reinforced by special services. It makes us all see ourselves rather differently as well. If we all share common feelings, strengths and weaknesses, then maybe we are more alike than we thought we were.

We are not too well equipped to deal with this notion. We are the inheritors, after all, of a long line of Utopian literature, and in those ideal societies dreamed of by philosophers down the ages, the point about disability is not that it is accepted as part of the human condition, but that it doesn't exist at all. The inhabitants of Utopias are whole in mind and body, sometimes even perfect in their understanding and beauty. Age brings only wisdom, not decay. Even where sickness and disability are admitted, they are not allowed to disrupt. Those who are sick are restored to health. Those who are incurably diseased in mind and body are destroyed, left to die or hidden away in hospitals or other places too secret to mention. Not for nothing did the citizens of Samuel Butler's satire *Erewhon* see sickness as a crime and punish the offence.

We know that we don't live in Utopia. We know that our modern societies are often hazardous places, that the price of our industries is often the disablement of their workers, that the by-product of modern medicine can be disability as well as health. We certainly don't intend to punish the casualties of this dangerous world. We have a notion of progress; we make provision. We even find cause for pride in our pluralism, in the variety that goes to make up the social mix.

But we are also societies that like to keep things orderly. We sort our apples to remind nature that variety is all very well, but what we want is a standard product. We are even working on the square tomato which will so neatly slot into our square storage arrangements. We are societies which pride ourselves on our efficiency, productivity and material progress; we haven't much time to waste on those of our members who fall short of the competence we demand. We know that physical perfection exists only on the advertising posters; but we keep on buying the wares they offer. We slap on cosmetics against the reality of physical imperfection and decay. We turn to this food fad and that, to build ourselves against weakness. We jog away the reality that by the time we are seventy, a quarter of us, if we are women, and a fifth of us, if we are men, can expect to be categorized as severely or appreciably disabled.

We resist the thought, above all, that in the imperfect bodies and minds of those already so categorized, we are seeing a mirror image of our own. We put away the thought and we put away the people. The deliberately segregationist policies of the past may have given way to notions of 'community care'; 'deinstitutionalization' may be a major thrust of the social policies of our Western societies. But there is enough in the experience of their workings in practice to show that the old attitudes linger on, however modified the ways in which they are expressed.

Nor are these attitudes, and these expressions of them, simply something exercised by an 'able' majority against a 'disabled' minority. 'I feel a fool and an idiot when I am walking,' says a woman whose right arm and leg are affected by multiple sclerosis.

In fact, I feel that if I did not feel this way I would walk better. I find I watch other people to see if there is any fault in their walk. When people are walking towards me, I see their eyes slide away at first, and each time I'm pleased, then angry — pleased that they care and don't want to embarrass me further, then angry that they need to look away, so I can't be attractive at all, no matter how I dress. I have a wild desire that a movie film could be taken of me walking, so that I could try to improve myself — then I think that I couldn't bear to watch, in case I look worse than I think I do. I also still feel uncomfortable with other disabled people, because I feel about them as I think normal people feel about me.

A man who has got about in a wheelchair for over four years still prefers to avoid the places where he might meet people he knows. He finds the sight of others in wheelchairs 'rather pathetic'; although pathetic is the last thing he feels himself to be, he wonders sometimes if that is the way that people see him. We are all in this together, bound by the same notion of the 'norm', the same urge to turn away from, or at least manage tidily, its transgression. These too are part of our common experience.

And yet there is nothing to say that the package that makes up the 'normal' is immutable. It has changed from time to time and place to place, and it is changing now. An isolated tribe in West Africa, for instance, has a genetic quirk which means that a large proportion of its children are born with two large toes on each foot instead of five, so that instead of a 'normal' foot, they have a sort of claw; sometimes they have webbing between their fingers as well. But there is nothing 'abnormal' about these children; they are not seen as disabled. Children, in this society, are accepted as coming with either four toes or ten, and neither variety is expected more than the other; all the children grow up to be full and equal members of the tribe. Legend has it that when the first four-toed child was born, many generations ago, it was put to death. So was the second. But when the third arrived, the tribe decided that it was meant. So it extended its concept of the 'normal' to accept it and the others who were born later.

We don't have to go as far as an isolated African tribe to see this process of redefinition at work. Left-handedness, for instance, has long been associated with the powers of darkness and evil. In practical terms, this has meant that, until fairly recently, British children who naturally started to write with their left hands were 'changed'; the proper hand for writing was the right one. Yet that would hardly happen today. Left-handed people are counted as among the 'normals' of our society.

8

More dramatically, in 1949/50, the British medical journal *Lancet* ran a sensitive series of first-hand accounts of living with disability. This covered, among many other topics, heart disease, paraplegia, polio, cerebral palsy — and an account by a lesbian woman of her life and feelings. Homosexuality may not yet be fully accepted as part of the run of 'normal' behaviour; homosexuals still meet discrimination. But they would hardly expect, and they would not be asked, to contribute to a series on disability today.

Just as societies can change to bring what has seemed 'abnormal' into their accepted range of 'normality', so can they change to exclude people who were once included in that range. It was only when universal education was introduced in England at the end of the last century, for instance, that it became expected that every child would learn to read and write. And it was only when this became a 'normal' expectation that people who found it hard, or even impossible, to master this skill became defined as 'disabled' — in this case, 'mentally defective'. The woman who all her life has been known as mentally handicapped isn't making a stupid distinction when she says, 'I'm not mental, it's just that I can't read and write'. She is actually challenging a norm which her society has held for only a hundred years.

The redefinitions continue. They are at work in the post-war build-up of special education in Britain, which means that more and more children have been excluded from ordinary schools, in no less than eleven major catcogries, in spite of official intentions to include as many of them as possible in that 'normal' framework. They are operating in the 'mainstreaming' policies of the United States, which aim to adapt the educational norm as far as possible to the needs of children hitherto excluded from it because of disabilities. They are at work in individual lives, as people are defined by the places they find themselves in. As one young American says: 'They didn't call me retarded outside, just here in the institution. Outside, no one knew. You act like they act — no one knows you're retarded. The only way they'll know you're retarded is if they're told by someone else.'[3]

So there is nothing immutable about the 'normal' range of

abilities and inabilities. We can and do change it, either to draw its boundaries more closely, and exclude more and more people as 'abnormal', or to widen those boundaries increasingly to include them. If we do the second, we will modify our ordinary social institutions so that they can accept a wider range of ability and inability in the people who use them. If we do the first, we will, in our humanitarian concerns, construct ever more elaborate separate systems to manage more and more people as 'different'.

Which we choose matters critically to people with disabilities, for their experience is the product not simply of their individual bodies, hearts and heads, but of the situations they find themselves in. In the past, it is they who have carried the responsibility for fitting into 'normal' social patterns. There has been little thought that these patterns should adapt to encompass them. Today, the inability of certain people to do certain 'normal' things is still seen as *their* handicap, a consequence of their disability. The first official aim of the International Year of Disabled People in 1981 was 'helping disabled people in their physical and psychological adjustment to society'. The real question is a different one. How far is society willing to adjust its patterns and expectations to include its members who have disabilities, and to remove handicaps that are now imposed on their inevitable limitations?

In this book, a disability is something that has to be taken as given. But a handicap is something that is imposed on that disability to make it more limiting than it must necessarily be. Obviously, to take just one example, people whose spine has been broken in certain places will be unable to walk, and just as obviously that will impose considerable limitations on what they can do. But just how handicapping those limitations are will depend on all sorts of factors that have to do not with the individuals but with the environment they find themselves in. It will depend on whether they can find a wheelchair that suits their needs, on whether the places they live in are so organized that they can reach what they need to control them, on whether they are faced with flights of steps between themselves and the places they want to get to, on how others respond to the fact that they can't stand or walk. How prepared are we to alleviate

10

the handicaps?

The answer matters to us all, and not just because one day those of us who do not reckon to have a disability might join those who already do. It matters because it will say a great deal about the tolerance that our societies have for any human differences, any human weaknesses, any human failure to meet their increasingly complex demands. And in saying that, it will say something about our understanding of the essential thread of experience that binds us all into a common humanity, whatever our individual quota of ability and inability. If we reject that common experience, it is, in the end, a part of ourselves that we are rejecting. If we accept it, we could all find ourselves a little nearer wholeness.

The next section starts teasing out that common thread of experience, as well as some of the factors that handicap us in our understanding of it and of each other as well. But first, the air needs to be cleared of some basic misconceptions, which are handicapping in themselves. We look at these in the next chapter.

2

Whose Problem?

A group of young people, three or four of whom had visible handicaps, mental and physical, were working in the garden of the community to which they all belonged. They seemed to be enjoying themselves and each other; they were chatting and laughing as they worked. They were evidently doing a good job – the garden offered the particular delights of sight and smell that well-tended vegetable gardens do, and the promise of nourishment to come. It was a beautiful, sunny day. The middle-aged visitor looked at this scene and sighed. 'Isn't,' she said, 'it sad?'

Well, is it?

A girl of eighteen is planning her career. She hopes to study the history of art and eventually to work in an art gallery or craft shop, although she is not naive about just how few jobs there are about. In the meantime, her life is good. She has a large circle of friends; she enjoys her schoolwork, as well as reading and listening to music; she does some drawing and poetry-writing. She has no urge for sports or rock-climbing, so the fact that all her life she has worn surgical boots and walked with crutches doesn't seem too much of a problem to her. She doesn't feel herself to be 'sad' – far from it. She feels accepted for who she is, and that she has been much helped through life by the 'many small children who stare at my crutches and watch, fascinated, as I walk'. She usually sums up by saying she's not an invalid – it's just that she can't walk unaided.

Another girl, also eighteen, remembers the summer, four years ago, as particularly precious. That was the year she did outstandingly well in sport. It was also the last year of her sporting life, because she was found to have a cancer and had to have one of her legs amputated. The loss can still hurt.

Feelings always remain concealed where sport is concerned; I rely on memory to combat this injustice. This is the area which can move me most, although I can contain my cries. I have since abandoned sport except for some table-tennis. I suspect that I am afraid to try anything that will confirm my immobility. I always keep within the limits, in this way I protect myself. I face reality, but I avoid the parts of reality that can be rejected.

Most of the time, though, she is looking forwards, not backwards. She can laugh at herself, she reckons she will do well in the business career she plans. 'It all comes down to the basic idea that many people find it difficult to accept that disabled people can lead a "normal" fulfilling life. Once people accept that you don't want to turn your face to the wall and opt out, it will be easier to break down the forbidding barriers.' She is getting a bit tired, too, of her elders who besiege her with tales of people with one leg who go mountaineering and perform other feats of physical strength. Who, she wonders, would ever think of telling people with two legs about other people with two legs who climb mountains? She can see that people are trying to encourage her. But she resents the 'assumed grouping'. What she wants is to be seen as herself.

A middle-aged man remembers his first reaction to discovering he had polio. 'I was desperate, desolate, depressed. I don't know where all the tears came from; I saw no future — either professionally, or as a husband, father or anything else.' As he recovered, he had to learn to cope with life from a wheelchair, with the fact that he would always need help to move from it to lavatory or bed. He had to start building again a professional career which had seemed irrevocably shattered. He managed, finally, to get a job, and although he still has moments of comparing his status with that of contemporaries, it is a pretty good one. His marriage did not collapse; he has the satisfaction of seeing his daughter grown up and happily settled, with a child of her own. He found his future.

A local government officer had to give up his job when his sight finally became so bad that he became registered as blind. He worked for five more years, helping to find jobs for adolescents who were blind themselves. Then he noticed that he had started to stagger as he walked; he was diagnosed as having multiple sclerosis. He is now confined to a wheelchair, paralysed from the waist down, and he has no sight at all. He rarely goes out – there doesn't seem much point to him in going for a drive if you can't see where you are going. He spends most of his time in the room he has had fixed up to meet his needs. His life could be counted hard, he reckons, if he compared it to that of his able contemporaries. But he doesn't. He feels released from the materialistic and competitive rat-race; he is not constrained by the need to earn a living in a job he dislikes. He has the time to reflect, write and read. He is convinced that everybody can lead a full and happy life – he only wishes that more people with disabilities got more encouragement to do so. 'It's an attitude of mind. You can have the same happiness or depression whether you're poor or severely disabled or whether you've got nothing at all to worry about. The mind adjusts itself to make equality among all people. Life is what you make it.'

We all know people who seem to have all possible gifts except the capacity to enjoy them. We all know, too, people who seem to have very little working for them and yet who radiate happiness. There are people who seem constantly to be striving for something beyond what they have already; there are others who seem simply to get on with what they've got. The general contentment of others again is punctuated by moments of yearning for something else, the more haunting, perhaps, for that something being almost undefinable. Among those people we will recognize ourselves. We all live by either 'asset values' – enjoying what we have – or 'comparative values' – looking over our shoulders to see what the next person has that we haven't. In *Physical Disability: a Psychological Approach*, Beatrice Wright has suggested that people with physical disabilities might find it useful to opt for the first; the same could be said to us all. For all of us, life is the business of reconciling our dreams and our realities, what is 'normal' for us, and some of us will do so more happily than others.

That has nothing to do with whether or not we have an obvious disability. In her review of the literature on its psychology, Beatrice Wright has been able to explode four myths. Most people with physical disabilities, she finds, makes about as good or as poor an adjustment as people without them; there is nothing to support the view that they are generally 'maladjusted', and that is because they, like anyone, are human beings and not objects 'which become more and more scarred with each successive blow'. Their life is not a 'tragedy', although the event that brought their disability may be; they, like anyone, can refocus their values to live where they are. They are not excessively frustrated, for much the same reason. Nor are they more overwhelmed with shame and guilt than anyone else.

So if the onset of a disability can seem to signal the end of everything that people value and enjoy, it need not. In *Journey into Silence,* Jack Ashley recounts his experience of becoming totally deaf. He remembers the realization that he was wholly excluded from the conversation of his wife and brother-in-law as they drove him home from hospital as 'one of the greatest shocks of my life'. When he first tried to get back to work, to a job in which quick understanding and discussion are essential, he realized that he was unable to participate at all. 'I was cut off from mankind, surrounded by an invisible, impenetrable barrier. I could see people clearly, but they belonged to a different world — a world of talk, of music and laughter.' His personal world, as he was to discover, was one in which music was replaced by a constant clanking and grinding, as if a fleet of Liverpool trams was running through his head. He had to give up aspirations of reaching the top of his career ladder. But his old life was not destroyed. He is still a Member of Parliament, working energetically in the interests of people with disabilities.

A disability can bring not just an end to one pattern of life, but a beginning of a new one. An ex-miner couldn't imagine not spending every evening in the club or going for long walks; he is now a teetotal non-smoker as the result of a severe heart condition, and gets about in a wheelchair because he has had a leg amputated. But he says he has never enjoyed his life more. He has taken up archery and painting, and reckons that his chairbound birdwatching, sketching and photographic excursions have taken his wife and himself over a thousand miles. 'When you go to bed, always have something for tomorrow to anticipate, a looking forward to another enjoyable day. Make little of your disability to other people and, most important, keep your sense of humour.'

Disability can bring new perspectives — a recognition of what real friendship means, a heightened sense of the preciousness of life, the lasting strength that comes from a religious experience at the point of death, which is no less real for being nameless. It can bring new opportunities, as it did to a man who was paralysed in a swimming accident and reckons that he would never have got himself a higher education and a foothold in academia unless his life had taken this turn.

Then again, disability can bring a narrowing of life and its pleasures. A woman in her seventies who has severe arthritis reckons herself lucky to have had a full and interesting life, and to have plenty to occupy her still. 'My mother and aunt kept their clocks an hour fast because it made time go more quickly. I have too much to do each day and the weeks fly!' But still, she adds: 'I dare not indulge in nostalgia. I dare not remember how I once walked miles with a long, swinging stride. I dare not remember how I lay, until two years ago, every night in a hot bath. Now I sit on a board and let the nurse wash me and pour water over myself from a small saucepan!' For some people, disability may mean that what is present offers no compensations for what is past. A woman who also has severe arthritis and lives alone after thirty years of the busy life of a shop finds that the worst aspect of her life is 'waking each morning and knowing that you have another day of frustration facing you, and that you can no longer plan ahead for days out and holidays. It is like living in one's own little world, living in the past rather than being able to look forward.'

For some people, what is present does not amount to a life at all. A middle-aged woman, chairbound by arthritis, has a good job and her own house. But, she says:

None of what goes on in the real world seems relevant to me, everything I see or hear about concerns activities from which I am barred. In fact, I am disconnected from life, because I am no longer a living human being. Occasionally I can forget this, when I am working, reading or listening to the radio, but it is only a brief escape. The worst is when I wake up in the morning, as when I am dreaming I walk about and do the things I used to do, and have to come back to the fact that I will never do any of it again. I think that there is only one solution, and that is termination of this non-life which is a burden and an embarrassment to the community and is cruel to the sufferers. I should not have been allowed to wake up from my third operation, and people like me, for whom there is no hope of improvement or of a reasonably liveable existence should not have to drag on in fear and pain, or risk worse by trying to put an end to it themselves. To all intents and purposes I died then, and the thing that does not look, let alone feel, like me should not be allowed to add to the other ugly things of life, but should be humanely and unobtrusively disposed of.

For others again, disability is a fact of life, not death, a fact to be lived with in all its complexity. A young woman with a progressive neuro-muscular disease remembers her capitulation to sticks and a wheelchair.

The previous 'active' year had been spent in such a haze of effort, pain and weakness that when I finally could not try any more, the resultant inactivity was a relief. Then the full horror of frustration and dependence hit me and I went through a few months of self-pity and expecting others to make life easier for me. I finally came through with the realization that life was going to be tough but that I had to cope with it myself, keeping my dependence on others down to a minimum and making my life as interesting as possible within the confines of disability.

There is nothing in these glimpses of living with disability to say that it must be 'tragic'. The *event* that leads to disability

17

may be; the life that stems from it need not, for each individual will bring to it his or her own quota of individual beliefs, abilities and strengths. Each of us lives in our own way with what is 'normal' for us.

Yet the contention that disability is a lasting personal tragedy can be drummed home every day. Pick up a professional journal and you can read about a young man who is 'suffering' from Down's Syndrome. Pick up a newspaper and you can read an article about the British Voluntary Euthanasia Society which features a young man who was determined to kill himself and only failed because his battery-powered wheelchair obstinately stuck within inches of the river bank. Pick up that same newspaper a week later and you can read a letter from a professional counsellor who contends that, however dire and depressing people feel their lives to be, they can always make some choices — unless, that is, they are 'physically handicapped or under lock and key'.

The literature on the psychology of disability can make contention fact. We can read the results of any number of abstruse professional studies which show that children with disabilities have unrealistic goals, compulsive behaviour, rigidity of personality and a distorted body image; that adults who acquire a disability in later life go through a period of shock, mourning, depression and the experience of internalized failure. The four common myths that Beatrice Wright felt it necessary to explode were not picked out of the air; it was from the professional literature that she culled the notions that people with disabilities are in general maladjusted, that their experience is of tragedy, that they suffer from excessive frustration and a sense of guilt.

We can learn, too, that the birth of a child with a disability is a tragedy not only for that child, but for its family. Hannah Mussett writes in *The Untrodden Ways* about her daughter Lucy, who has Down's Syndrome. 'There is in life sometimes, suffering so great as to make us for ever resist the imagining, and where a babe new-born is already destined to live to this, there does not seem to me to be any justification for denying it the mercy of a swift and painless death.' She recounts her own anguish as she struggles between her desire to kill the

18

child and the social pressures which, she feels, compel her to cherish it; she lays bare her own torn instincts and the damage that is done to family life by Lucy's presence. 'Show me a handicapped child and I'll show you a handicapped family.' The literature can bear her out. Parents react to the birth of a child with a disability with shock, denial, grief, anxiety, fright and horror, as well as guilt, shame and acute embarrassment when they are with other people. Its presence brings isolation to its mother, as well as physical and mental ill-health to her and often to the father as well, and problems to brothers and sisters on top of that; the divorce rate among these parents is far higher than among others.

Yet there was nothing at all in the article about the young man with Down's Syndrome to suggest that he was 'suffering' from this chromosomal accident. The article was about a battle between his parents and the local authority over where he should live, and if he was 'suffering' from anything, it was from that. The member of the Voluntary Euthanasia Society quoted in the newspaper was totally atypical of its membership; indeed, the Society could not remember more than one other young person with a similar disability who had approached it within months of the article's publication. To suggest, as the counsellor did, that people with physical disabilities cannot make choices is evidently rubbish – they, like everyone else, do so every day.

If the literature on physical disability can seem to produce a catalogue of sorrows, there is the experience of individuals to challenge its inevitability. Some people at least who are paralysed as a result of a spinal injury will say that they reacted to their new condition not with the mourning and depression that the textbooks describe, but with a determination to get on with their new life. One man remembers his initial experience of polio as an almost privileged release from any expectations or desires or strivings; it was only when he was told that his time in the rehabilitation unit was up, after a year of treatment, that he was shocked and angered with the realization that he would not, after all, recover the full use of his legs.

And if Hannah Mussett's experience of having a child with a disability is nothing but grief and pain, there is the reaction

19

of Nicola Schaefer to pit against it. In *Does She Know She's There?*, she describes her feelings on learning that her daughter Catherine, her first child, has profound disabilities, both mental and physical. 'This is a lousy blow we've been dealt, but what's the point of moaning and moping? I'll accept and enjoy Catherine for what she is and take things step by step and not worry about the future for the time being.' And so she did, and her account of the family's life with Catherine is warm and funny and loving — a real celebration. The literature as well as the experience of countless parents shows that life with a child with a disability is very far from unmitigated horror, that isolation has to do more with the personality of the mother than with anything else, that along with the sorrow and the strains comes at least the usual quota of delight and enjoyment, simply because each one of us is our own mixture of abilities and inabilities, each one of us is more than the categorization we may have attracted.

So why the assumption of continuing 'tragedy'? Why, when we all know and respect the final impossibility of complete understanding of what makes up the 'normality' of anyone other than ourselves, the assumption that we understand personal normality in people we have never met?

The obverse, the notion that disability need not be tragic, is a dangerous one to our Western societies. If people can enjoy life when they so obviously fall short of that elusive 'norm' towards which we all, consciously or unconsciously, strive, then what is our striving worth? If they, in their obvious 'imperfection', may actually seem within touch of what we recognize as happiness and fulfilment, then what imperfections in us are blocking our way? If they, in their possible economic 'uselessness' nevertheless have a sense of their own worth, then what of the values of materialism? Paul Hunt, who himself lived and died with muscular dystrophy, makes the point in 'A Critical Condition':

> Severely disabled people are generally considered to have been unlucky, to be deprived and poor, to lead cramped lives. We do not enjoy many of the 'goods' that people in our society are accustomed to . . . If the worth of human

beings depends on a high social status, on the possession of wealth, on a position as a parent, husband or wife — if such things are *all-important* — then those of us who have lost or never had them are indeed unfortunate. Our lives must be tragically upset and marred for ever, we must be only half alive, only half human . . . But set over against this common sense attitude is another fact, a strange one. In my experience even the most severely disabled people retain an ineradicable conviction that they are still fully human in all that is ultimately necessary. Obviously each person can deny this and act accordingly. Yet even when he is most depressed, even when he says he would be better off dead, the underlying sense of his own worth remains.

The challenge is not a comfortable one The 'norm' demands that people whose disabilities are obvious and severe must be at least 'sad' and even 'tragic'. And if that defence breaks down in the face of individual reality, it is ready with its own flip-side. The reaction to people who break out of the mould becomes: 'Aren't they wonderful?'

So in the United States there is an award for the Handicapped Person of the Year, which in 1979 went to a Vietnam veteran who had lost the sight of one eye and had both legs and his lower left arm amputated. He is, nevertheless, a very accomplished rider and hopes to set up a ranch where people with severe disabilities can learn the same skills, to the point where a party of them can negotiate their way to the bottom of the Grand Canyon on horseback. So in Britain, the Spastics Society has been making its special achievement award since 1972. In 1978 it went to a man who, despite his very severe disabilities — he is unable to eat unaided, dress himself or walk, and his speech is impaired — has set up a cultural centre for people with disabilities, a playgroup for handicapped children and a telephone club which has five hundred members.

Just as it is not in any way to deny the reality of individual tragedy to question the myth of its inevitability, it is not in any way to belittle individual achievement to point out that 'Aren't They Wonderful?' is in its way as pernicious as its reverse. What it does is to confirm the rule by singling out the

21

apparent exception. As Paul Hunt says: 'The "unfortunate" person is assumed to have wonderful and exceptional courage . . . This devalues other people by implication, and leaves the fit person still with his original view that disablement is really utterly tragic.' This is as true if the person singled out for praise is the person who lives with someone with a disability. If their mothers, wives or husbands are 'wonderful' for coping, where does that leave the people who have the disability?

It leaves them with a problem. And the question that needs to be asked is how far that problem is their own and how far they are carrying it for other people. People who have a disability must live with it; it is their 'normality'. How they live with it will have to do not just with their individual qualities, but with the situation they find themselves in; they are not somehow 'different' from anyone else in that, either. And while disability is a 'given', the handicaps that come from the behaviour of other people and the attitudes that lie behind it are not ineradicable.

The realization that your parents wish you were other than you are has a powerful effect on any child; we can all see the results of small acceptances and rejections in our own lives. What can it mean to understand that your parents, too, see you as somehow 'sad'? One young woman remembers a pilgrimage to Lourdes, when she was about eight, to pray for the miracle that would make whole her dwarfed and twisted body. She remembers her own dawning understanding, as yet inexpressible, that the search for 'cure' was not for her, that this was her body to live with, her 'normality'. The realization was something to hang on to through her adolescence, when her 'tragedy' could threaten to overwhelm her. For a young man who is mentally retarded, the sense that his parents found him a disappointment was more damaging. When he came home from one of those 'special' sporting events, in which every race is a caucus race and everyone gets a prize, duly bearing his medal, he asked: 'Now, do you think my mother will believe that I'm worth something?' Hannah Mussett remained convinced that her failure to kill her daughter Lucy, like her failure to put an end to a rabbit she once came across in a trap, was a measure of her weakness, not her strength; she

22

remained convinced that her daughter's life was a tragedy. But what we learn about Lucy throughout the book was that she was developing as a happy child — slowly, but with her own distinctive likes, dislikes and sense of her own person. Whose problem?

The assumptions can throw up powerful barriers between people as they go about their lives. 'Aren't you wonderful?' may be easier to live with than the gush of uneasy sympathy that comes with 'Aren't you sad?', and even seductive in its flattery. But it is no nearer who you are. A woman who was born without a right forearm is tired of hearing how 'wonderful' she is to cope, and even how fortunate she must feel that she wasn't born right-handed. She is more than irritated by the consequence of this attitude, which is that she isn't 'allowed' to have any problems at all. Once docketed as 'wonderful', wonderful is what you must be; if once you challenge that, you can find yourself ending up 'sad'. So another woman says:

No one likes slipping on a banana skin, likes constantly calling attention to themselves. But all the disabled stick out in a crowd. My husband often has to carry me. A friend said, 'How good of you not to mind!' Not mind! I hate it. But it has to be done, otherwise I would have to stay at home. It is hard work carrying off indignity with dignity.

So another woman says that she gets no sympathy for the sort of emotional and financial problems that could hit anyone; they are all seen as part of her disability, and what can she expect? So another feels that any ordinary show of irritation will immediately be put down not to the event which produced it, but to her disability: 'Poor thing, it must be so hard for her!'

Attitudes don't just hang in the air; they are expressed in and reinforced by behaviours. If people are perceived as 'sad', then there is not much point in offering them much change in their situation, for whatever happens, sad is what they will remain. And that response will, in its turn, begin to colour the way that people live with their own individual 'normality'. This is how life seems to a woman who has had multiple sclerosis for the past fourteen years.

They don't like the word cripple. Disabled. A rose by any other name. I'm a cripple. I can't walk or stand or run or dance or anything. God, I hate it. So I am resentful, bitter, nasty and why the hell shouldn't I be? Who understands? They come up with platitudes, shit about 'I know just how you feel'. How the hell does anyone know just how I feel? Of course it hasn't affected my mind, but I wish to God it would, because then I wouldn't feel so depressed about it. It just slowly kills everything. It started with my left foot. I couldn't walk in my sling-back stilettos. It then went travelling down my left leg, then it started on my left hand, then it went on to my eyes. Now I'm left in a wheelchair with no feeling in my legs . . . My hands shake, they shake terribly. I can't read any more because the lines in the sentence don't stay still . . . You wouldn't mind, but it didn't hit me until I was 20, so I know what dancing, walking, flirting, standing was . . . You fight it, my God, you fight it, but it wins, it wins in the end . . . I must find a place somewhere, but since it happened, I just don't seem to fit anywhere. I just want somewhere I can belong, somewhere with other people of my age, and then maybe I wouldn't wallow so much in self-pity. At the moment, I seem to be fighting the world alone and it gets lonely. God, it gets so lonely. I've just got to feel part of something, somebody who needs and wants me. It's very important, you know. We think we're so hard, but everybody does need someone, just one person who you can be close to and share everything with. I'm not talking about sex — wouldn't be much bloody point anyway. I just want somewhere, people my own age who would understand, who know what it's like.

Her individual tragedy is, in the end, to be respected as hers to live with. But what she is asking for is a place to live that is neither the hospital ward she is in now nor a residential home in which everyone else is twice her age: what she is asking for is the opportunity of relationship. And these are requests which demand a practical response.

Attitudes and the behaviour that follow them don't affect just individuals. They affect whole groups of people. As they move about their community, people with physical disabilities meet not just a barrage of physical barriers in the shape of steps and unadapted spaces, but a whole host of rules and regulations as well. The thinking behind many of these hardly stands up to scrutiny. Why does 'safety' demand that a blind person is accompanied in theatres and cinemas, when he or she is the one person who could give lessons to the rest of the audience on what to do if the lights fuse? What is so 'safe' about the ruling that people in wheelchairs must transfer into ordinary theatre seats, when in any situation that called for speedy reaction they would lose vital time in transferring back to the chairs that can propel them as fast as other people's legs may do them? There is little that is rational in the regulations. But perhaps there is little that is rational in the attitudes behind them. If people with disabilities are 'sad', if their situation is tragic, what use have they for the ordinary pleasures of life? 'We're not meant to enjoy ourselves', says one young man ruefully. He would not be the first to find that people react with something like shock when his friends haul him in his wheelchair up the stairs to the disco. 'We're not', as he says, 'supposed to like that sort of thing.'

The bars can be more explicit than that. As the manager of one dance hall said: 'What is the point in fighting for the right to go dancing, when in point of fact, hardly any of them can go dancing or want to go dancing?' And as the manager of a menswear shop put it, when asked about its inaccessibility to people in wheelchairs: 'As a young fashion store, we are hardly the place one would expect to find people in wheelchairs frequenting. Our merchandise is essentially aimed at the young, slim and active'.[1] The young, slim and chairbound clearly have no business at all to be fashion-conscious as well; what point, after all, in dressing like their contemporaries when their 'sadness' dictates that they cannot behave like them? The risk of that 'sadness' contaminating others cannot be run. The chain of British holiday camps which bars from its dining rooms people who need to be fed, even if they bring with them all the helpers they need, doesn't want, it says, to 'distress' the

25

other customers. After all, as the man said, we offer a family holiday — even though parties of people with disabilities tend to go in the very months that families can't. And after all, we must understand that there is a lot going on in these camps, that many of the activities are hardly the sort that people with very severe disabilities would enjoy.

From time to time, in their relationships with those they meet, people with disabilities will be able to break out of the mould they so often find themselves in. They will be told: 'But I never think of you as disabled!' They no longer fit the stereotype; they are no longer seen as 'sad' or 'wonderful' simply because they have a disability. They are no longer lumped into a preconceived grouping, but are seen as individuals.

For some people, like the woman who counts it a compliment when people so far forget her disability as to pass her something that her hands are too weak to hold, this means acceptance. For others, like the young man who, when he left his special school, felt he had also left behind his categorization for ever, to take his place in the 'normal' world, it could be the thing they most want to hear. But for him now, and for very many people, this is no longer enough. Their disabilities are part of their 'normality', a fact of their lives with which they must live more or less happily, more or less angrily, more or less sadly. Just how they will live will depend not simply on their individual resources, but on how the society to which they belong can adapt to accommodate them and the limitations they bring with them. We are all in this together; the 'problem' of disability is not for isolated individuals, a personal 'tragedy', but one in which we all have a part. Responses to that mutual problem in the context of the family and the wider world are what the next three chapters are about.

3

Family Matters

The Smiths would not, probably, count themselves as very extraordinary. They know that in some ways they are extremely fortunate. Mr Smith has a responsible job which he is known to do well: 'recognition by my peers is my good fortune'. They have enough money to make the practical adjustments which their circumstances demand and no major financial worries for the future. They and their four teenage children are very close — closer, they agree, than they might have been if those circumstances had been different. As Mr Smith says: 'I need them, and they recognize it.' They have a circle of friends of the sort who can be called 'extended family'. They know that they have a problem to cope with. But as Mrs Smith says: 'Our attitude has always been that we have no right to say, "Why should this happen?" and that there is much to be gained personally from overcoming the difficulties cheerfully.'

The difficulties, and the closeness too, are much coloured by the fact that Mr Smith has had rheumatoid arthritis for the past twenty years — since two years before he and his wife were married — and by the increasing physical limitations this brings. Some difficulties they have coped with as they have arisen — by handrails on the stairs, a shower unit instead of a bath, Mrs Smith's quiet opening of screwtop jars. Other difficulties have for so long been part of the pattern of family life that they aren't difficulties at all. When the children were very small, for instance, there was never any problem over clearing up their toys at bedtime, because they knew that this was important, not to satisfy their mother's notions of tidiness, but to ensure that their father didn't fall and hurt himself; they knew that theirs was simply not a house in which to play marbles carelessly. They knew too that difficulties in some areas of life don't mean difficulties in them all. They, like their parents, have a whole range of activities and interests in their community; they have learned that disability changes what you do rather than stopping you from doing things. When Mr Smith introduced his twelve-year-old son to his own old golf club, he said that he would like to be playing with him. His son replied: 'But Daddy, if you didn't have arthritis, then we wouldn't know what it was like to be fit.'

Sometimes the differences between the way the Smiths live and the way other families do can seem to bring more problems. Holiday times, Mrs Smith reckons, are the worst, because then there is more time to think, and then, too, most people are more physically active than they are for the rest of the year. She heard her youngest daughter tell a cousin on holiday last year: 'We don't go for walks' – and they don't, because they prefer to do things as a family. Sometimes Mr Smith feels that they should goad the children into more activity – but, then, as his wife says, he hates being left alone while the rest go off. But the problem is getting less as the children are growing up and doing more on their own anyway, leaving their mother to rejoice in holiday idleness after a year full of action. And if she knows that she relies on the children at times when Mr Smith's disability progresses a stage further and it's hard to adjust to this, they are both also quite determined that the children should grow up feeling free to live their own lives and not their parents'.

Some adjustments are harder than others. Mrs Smith gets irritated sometimes at always having to remember to leave much more time than usual to get anywhere, because of her husband's difficulties in getting in and out of the car. Travel away from home – of which he does a lot in the course of his work – is more difficult. He can't carry luggage, and finds it embarrassing to limp into an hotel followed by his wife carrying the bags; she counts herself strong and healthy, but she can find this very tiring. Rail travel would be easier if Mr Smith were more reconciled to using a wheelchair at stations. Life, in fact, could sometimes be easier all round if he used a chair. But, as his wife says: 'A combination of pride and his fear of the attitudes of other people to those in wheelchairs are making him put off the evil day as long as possible. So he would rather walk and risk the joints wearing out more quickly. I can't say I particularly want to push him round, but sometimes it would be the better of two evils.' As Mr Smith says himself: 'Like the driver speeding, I am not going to be caught! I am not going to be a cripple, I am going to be the exception. The extra handrail on the stairs, though vital, is another battle lost, but we will still win the war.'

Sometimes the difficulties can bring depression, though luckily it's rare that both of them are depressed at the same time, and their close friends are a tremendous help. Mr Smith reckons that it is far harder for his wife to watch his deterioration than it is for him, that it is harder to see pain than to have it. Mrs Smith finds her husband's deep fear of becoming a burden the worst problem of all. She doesn't know how she would react to her tall, handsome husband becoming totally crippled. They don't find it easy to talk to each other about these fears. But she has tried to explain that they will solve the problem, if it arises, somehow. 'On the whole, we have both learnt to take one week at a time. I can only believe that when the time comes (which I hope it will not) the strength to cope will also come.'

Every family in the land will find its own echoes in the Smith's patterns of coping; each family will have its own notion of what makes for a problem and the adjustments that have to be made to take it on board; each family will have its own patterns of friendship, its own working out of the complexities of dependence, independence and inter-dependence that make up living together. There is nothing to say that the patterns of families who have a disabled member must be different in *kind*, however different they may be in *degree*. Sometimes, indeed, they don't seem very different at all. In 'Marriage and the Handicapped', A.H. Sutton, who has severe cerebral palsy, describes his own family life:

My wife goes about her daily chores. I earn the living; we have friends who accept us; our bungalow is indistinguishable from the neighbouring bungalows except that possibly

29

ours is a little better kept. My wife helps me to dress; I help her to bath; we have sexual intercourse frequently; we row about my driving; she never has enough housekeeping money; she always lacks something to wear for that special occasion; in fact, it's all very normal.

Every family will have its own ways of bringing up the children and its own good reasons for these. Some parents clip their children over the ear; others are fervent disbelievers in physical punishment. One mother at least falls into the second category because she and her five-year-old both know that her inability to walk and limited use of her right hand rule out control by force. It surprises her that he hardly ever uses this trump card; but then she also knows that she is his mother and that the emotional level of their relationship has nothing to do with her disability: 'I have the same warmth and short-comings towards him as I would have had as an able-bodied mother.' There can't be many of those who haven't at some time, however fleetingly, just wished that their children would disappear and leave them in peace, or who have moments of wishing that they could somehow offer their children more than they do. They will hear echoes of themselves, perhaps, in the mother with very severe physical disabilities who says 'The little one is taken to the circus by her big sister; it hurts me, but I can't take her. I can't play with them and lift them up in the same way. I get nasty tempered and its seems unfair to them but I can't help it.' They may hear echoes in the experience of the woman who has had a thrombosis and reckons to suffer from 'nerves': 'I just can't sit with them or play with them. The difficulty is to settle down with them; because of my migraine my head is awful. I fall asleep half the time if I sit down. I'm never bright and cheery with them.'[1] They may even feel flashes of the distance between themselves and their babies that hit a woman who is blind when her daughter was tiny. The practical side of life she soon learned to cope with, and copes with still as its demands change. But the worst thing in the early days was when she only knew what her daughter was feeling when she cried.

She smiled, oh yes, she smiled frequently; people told me so, and what a lovely smile she had too, with those great dark eyes. And she often smiled at me, they said, fixing her eyes on me all the time. But I didn't know that when I was alone with her. You cannot hear a smile, only a cry. So there was no smile of pleasure when I dangled the teddy before her, or made mad faces, or even when I picked her up for the third time at dead of night. Just a cry, if I wasn't doing what she needed me to do at that time, or silence, which was almost worse, in a way.

As children grow up and become their own person, there can't be many parents who don't feel however faint an echo of the pang that hit another blind mother who realized that she would always be unable to share as closely as she'd like in the work that her children brought home from school. There can't be many children, either, who don't have their moments of wishing their parents were other than they are, of terror that family idosyncrasies will mark them out for ever in the conformist world that makes up school life. So while one mother with severe disabilities wonders how this will affect her son as he grows up, she has her husband on hand to remind her that he was mercilessly teased because he was the only boy in the school whose father was a vicar.

While each family lives its life in its own way, we have the realities behind the statistics on divorce and on children living away from their own homes to remind us that sometimes family life becomes intolerable, impossible to sustain. Children and adults with disabilities will be among those who make up the statistical totals. But again, there is nothing to say that they must inevitably end up there. There are studies of marriages among people who are mentally retarded to show that the realism they bring to their marriages, their instinctive sense of complementarity, their recognition of what they have to lose if the marriage breaks down, can make for more joy and fulfilment than ever came in the wake of a reliance on romance, and more long-lasting commitment as well. 'I was miserable before, no light of life or outside world,' says one husband, 'but I've got it now.' A wife puts it this way: 'I'm more happy now with a place of my own; I can go in and out when I like; this is our home.' Another couple makes the point: 'Each can sort the other's problems out, marriage is a wonderful life.' A man looks back over the years of his partnership: 'We never fall out — well, we do have words, but we fall in again.'[2]

But if there are factors that bring together families with a disabled member and families without them, there are also the factors that may make them different from each other. It is 'normal' to cope with a very young child who is highly active, doubly incontinent and unable to talk, whose delight in exploration gets its vent in pulling apart everything she can lay hands on. It is not 'normal' to cope when that child is still highly active, doubly incontinent and unable to talk, still has the same delights in exploration, but is now fourteen-years-old. To learn that her parents have not slept through a night for years, because the girl will only settle when she is in their room and even then barely sleeps herself, to hear of their helplessness faced with this behaviour, is only to touch on the degree of adaptation that this family has had to make to its 'normal' expectations. It is 'normal' for every family to hit an illness in a child which, for a short time, disrupts their ordinary patterns of living and limits what they can do. It is not 'normal' to have a child who is dying by inches from a brain tumour and has been slowly deteriorating for eight years, until at fourteen he looks like a little wizened old man, barely responsive to a touch on his cheek. To compare him now to the laughing photograph of the beautiful child he used to be, to hear his mother talk of him then and now, to hear the bitterness of her isolation, is only to touch on her sorrow. These may be extreme examples, but the mother of a child who is mentally retarded summed it up for many others when she said: 'Nobody is unsympathetic, but nobody understands.' A child with a severe disability is bound to be more dependent and for longer than a child without one; the limits on what is possible for that child may become limits on what is possible for the family. The restrictions can become so much part of the everyday experience of the family that it forgets things could be otherwise. 'No matter how handicapped the child is,' says one mother, 'I think you play it down to yourself a lot because

32

you have to live with it, and you get so used to living with it that you forget how badly handicapped your child is and how restricted your life is.'[3] Sometimes, the realization of the 'abnormality' of life can hit, when the pattern is briefly broken. 'I feel lost without her, somehow,' says a mother about her fifteen-year-old daughter who has severe cerebral palsy and is also mentally retarded.

> When we went on holiday, they took her into hospital for two weeks. Well, we only had a week's holiday and that week I was at home I didn't know what to do. I was sat here having my meal and I hadn't Gail to feed, no nappies to wash. It was a break, but I've got that used to it I just felt lost somehow, I just sat here with nothing to do.[4]

At the limit, the strains can become intolerable to the family. The child will go into some sort of residential care; the family itself may break down, leaving one parent to carry on alone.

When the member of the family who has a severe disability is not a child, but an adult, the differences between what is 'normal' for them and what is normal for the majority can seem greater yet. It is perfectly usual for any adult to have a spell of illness which brings a degree of, or even total, physical dependence. But it is quite 'abnormal' – except for the person concerned – for that dependence to last for years, even a lifetime. Yet that, inevitably, is what disability may mean. And that can be hard to live with.

It can be hard for the person with a disability, in the disruption it brings to 'ordinary' expectations of family life. One woman, left fairly weak by polio, reckons that the hardest part of her disability is having to rely so much on her elderly mother, when it would be usual, given their respective ages, for help to be going in the opposite direction. The greatest current worry of a man more severely disabled after the same disease is that he simply cannot give a son's 'normal' help to his own elderly parents, living at the other end of the country. The strains of dependence can be the greater the more nearly they touch essential relationships. 'Dependence is worse than pain,' says an elderly woman who dreads having to wake her husband for help in the night after a lifetime's belief in the value of enough sleep for everyone. 'A request to, or rebuff from, the State or a firm bothers me not a jot,' says one man.

I might quite enjoy a barney! Seeking a stranger's help in getting my wheelchair in and out of the car boot never bothers me either. But asking near and dear ones is more difficult than the sheer frequency factor ought to make it. It is almost impossible to separate emotional dependence from physical dependence and this must invariably fall on those close by. How can a disabled bloke who needs help to get to the toilet get there without some emotional disturbance? It always seems that the helper — usually my wife — is busy, shopping, deservedly snoozing over a TV programme or something equally unconducive. So what do you do? Stall for a while, hoping that telepathy really works and you won't need to ask? Cramp in bed's the same. Perhaps it shouldn't matter. But it does to me. An 'Oh, bloody hell!' from my wife is, although perfectly under-standable and only transitory, something which will screw me up more than fifty gaffes from others!

If the strains of living with an adult with a severe disability are less well documented than the strains where it is a child who has the disability that may be, as one wife suggests, because of the cloak of silence that surrounds the subject and is, for her, the hardest aspect of it. Any discussion of the strains too easily sounds like disloyalty to the person with a disability; while any mother can talk about the frustrations of being tied to a small child without being accused of lack of love, caring relatives have not, she reckons, reached that point. So they remain silent and are often brought to the point of breakdown by the endless small demands on their time — waiting always on the needs of the person with the disability, never able to suit themselves over the time they get up or go to bed, always being the one to queue at the bar, wondering incessantly what would happen if they should become ill. And if a wife — or caring husband or other relative — does pick up the courage to discuss the situation with a doctor or social worker, 'the response is, in general, something to the effect that she should be grateful for her own health and strength and an exhortation to keep cheerful for the sake of the disabled person'.[5]

So often the family has to reach complete exhaustion before it attracts any help at all. So a wife whose husband has Parkinson's disease, who feels compelled to watch him constantly to see that he doesn't fall, who has had to get up sometimes as often as seven times in a night, found herself too tired even to wheel his chair. It was only then that her doctor insisted that her husband spent two weeks in hospital to give her a break, and it was only as a result of that that they were offered more regular help. Sometimes, when help does come, it can be as bewildering to a family with an adult member with a disability as it can to the mother of a child. A man who had cared single-handedly for his wife for years simply didn't know what to do with the prospect of a free afternoon a week; he had to be coaxed into remembering his enjoyments in the days when he actually had time to pursue them. And sometimes, the strain of dependence can be too great and the family will break up completely. A woman with multiple sclerosis can understand what it must be like, she says, 'living with someone and seeing them just eaten away by this disease until they become so helpless, so dependent, so restricted in everything they try to do'. But she still hates her husband's guts for leaving her to live with a normally healthy woman who has borne his child.

The difficulties of living with someone with a severe disability, then, can be very different in degree from those of ordinary families. But just how limiting those difficulties become will depend not just on the families themselves, but on the circumstances they find themselves in. It will depend on how well their housing is adapted to their needs, for one thing, and on how much money they have, for another – we shall be looking at these factors later. It will also depend on how much help the families get.

And here is the second difference of degree between them and those whose difficulties fall within the range we call 'normal': while the second can find that there is no gap at all between their needs and the resources they can call on to meet them, or that the gap is perfectly liveable with, families with

35

a member with a disability can find that the gap is enormous. And because their needs are seen as 'abnormal', rather than an intensification of those all families have, they very easily get caught in the same trap as individuals with disabilities. If they cope without complaint − and the large majority of them do − they are seen as 'wonderful'. If they do point out their difficulties, they may find that they are labelled 'sad'; what else, after all, can they expect? Neither response brings them the help they need. So the limitations that disability brings become a problem not only for individuals, but for those closest to them as well. Just as a person with a disability is turned into a 'handicapped person', so his or her family is turned into a 'handicapped family', for whom the only solution is, at the limit, the temporary or permanent removal of the handicapped member, usually to a highly abnormal setting which offers no guarantee at all of meeting his or her real needs. The reality, which is that handicap is not inevitable, that families who live with disability are also families which have their share of 'normality' as well as 'abnormality', is forgotten. So is the fact that, given the right sort of help, they could live more of the first and less of the second. There must be a better way. There is, and its beginnings are to be found in all the services which take as their starting-point the need to bring help to people where they live, or at least in the most usual setting possible, and to ensure that that help is flexible enough to be tailored to individual need.

Families whose children's development is affected by disability will find that they have a whole variety of needs. The children will need an assessment by a number of professional workers, which goes further than diagnosis to specify what help they can use as well. In the past, their parents found the first − if at all − by trailing with their children from office to office, expert to expert, getting part of the story from each and sometimes help from none. Now, if they're lucky, they will find they can call on the sort of multi-disciplinary assessment offered in parts of the United States and elsewhere, which not only brings together all the professional experts but prescribes an Individual Programme Plan for the child which sets clear developmental goals and responsibility for reaching them.

Parents will want to feel that they too can help their child develop, just as they feel with any 'normal' child. In the past, they were probably told that nothing could be done, that the problem was theirs to live with. Now, if they're lucky, they can use one of the home teaching services, like those developed in West Germany, or through the Portage Project in Wisconsin, which teaches them to teach their child. Parents may also want to feel that they have the backing of people who really understand the difficulties they face. In they past, they may have felt nothing but isolation from the parents around them. Now, if they're lucky, they will be able to join one of the pilot-parent schemes, pioneered in the United States, which carefully match 'experienced' parents of children with developmental disabilities with 'new' ones, and offer the first the chance to bring the support to the second that no professional ever could.

And one of the other things that parents may want, especially as their child gets older, is a break. They may want it for themselves, and for their other children. But they may want it for their child with a disability as well, for it is 'normal', after all, for children as they get older to get away from their families from time to time, to stay over with friends, to extend their own horizons by taking a look at those of their contemporaries. In the past, that break usually meant one thing for families which could not draw on extensions of themselves: it meant admission to an institution which offered at worst bleak containment, at best a highly abnormal routine among strangers. It didn't offer so very much to parents either, for it would accept their child not when they needed the break, certainly not when they felt that they couldn't stand life a minute longer, but when it was good and ready by its own timetable. Now, if they're lucky, parents and children can use the sort of service offered by Extend-a-Family in Toronto, or by the different respite fostering schemes in England, which offer not only on-demand relief for parents, but the chance for their children to build a whole set of new friendships in the sort of environment they recognize — a family.

So the components for unravelling the handicaps that can wrap themselves round children with disabilities and their families are often there. There are just three problems. The first is that in some places they don't yet exist. The second is that parents don't know about them even if they do. And the third is that they can still be as beset by professional rivalries and uncoordinated in their approach as ever the old lack of services was deadening. A British research team sums up one aspect of this for one country: 'Home visits are carried out independently (and often without previous communication with others) by professionals from health, social services and education agencies. The managers of these agencies have separate responsibility for delivering a wide range of poorly specified and poorly monitored services of unknown effectiveness.' What families need now is the sort of service that draws together the components of help into a coherent whole, and knows why it is doing so.

In Britain, there is the beginning of a model in the child development centres, which are very slowly begining to spread a coordinated approach to helping children with disabilities and their families. In the United States there is, for instance, the work of the local offices of the Washington Bureau of Developmental Disabilities. It knows why it offers its home aid programme: 'Services are provided with the specific intent of eliminating or reducing the need for placing clients in residential settings which are more restrictive than the home/community environment.' It offers evaluation of the child's needs, and ensures that these are met – by doctor or dentist, physiotherapist, occupational, speech or behaviour therapist. Parents can learn to teach their child how to develop. They have their chance to get in touch with other parents whose older children have similar disabilities. They are offered regular as well as emergency short-term care for their children. The agency makes sure that they have the special equipment they need. And it has, by law, its own paid advocates to ensure that parents are getting the help that it is mandated to provide.

Services are seldom as good as they sound on paper. But what this and the other programmes set up across the United States under the developmental disabilities legislation have is a clear framework within which to offer help to families, with a clear reference point for parents who want that help. It is

38

not the components of the programme which are new, so much as the way they are brought together. Families whose children have disabilities need more of them.

The difficulties of a family with an adult member who has a disability may be of a different order. The uncertainty about the line and limits of development may be replaced by an uncertainty about the line and limits of deterioration. The initial diagnosis made, the fact established and rehabilitation therapy given, there may be very little uncertainty at all. Very often, the principal difficulty may be practical − the sheer and exhausting 'dailiness' of life for the carer. In Britain, there are district nursing and home help services to bring nursing and house-keeping relief into people's homes. But even if these are available, it is at their own time, in official working hours rather than when help may be most needed. There is even evidence that the patterns of official help actually make life harder for families, by disrupting their careful routines rather than supporting them. If families need a break from each other, there is usually only one way to get it: by sending the person with a disability into the abnormal and often uncongenial world of a hospital. And even then, the break usually only comes when the family has reached complete exhaustion. There must be a better way.

There is, and in Britain it is called Crossroads. Like all the best ideas, it is very simple, cuts straight through 'traditional' ways of doing things, and actually provides the help that families say they need instead of the help that providing agencies say they do. Very early on, the first Crossroads scheme made three fundamental discoveries. The first was that it is perfectly possible to provide families with the help they want at the time they want it. So a Crossroads care attendant will, for instance, go into someone's house very early in the morning to get them up and ready for work, and late at night to help them to bed − which is precisely the sort of demand that statutory services, bound to regular office hours, cannot meet. So a care attendant will sleep overnight, to ensure unbroken sleep for the carer on a couple of nights a week, at least. So an attendant enables a wife who has been caring for her husband for many years to do something as simple, yet put aside as an impossible luxury, as having her hair done once a week.

It is possible to provide this sort of flexible support, Crossroads has discovered, because people with very severe disabilities may actually only need a couple of hours' help a day, provided that it comes at critical times. And the third discovery is that it is possible to provide it with attendants whose training is simplicity itself, but no less revolutionary for that. They spend a month with the families to learn the routines that they, better than any professional worker, understand. Recruitment is not a problem, for if the work brings irregular hours and not always certain earnings, flexibility for the customers can mean flexibility for the attendant with – usually – her own family commitments as well.

By 1980, there were twenty Crossroads schemes in Britain, serving some 400 people and their families. The majority of them were elderly and all, because of the terms of its trust deeds, had physical disabilities. But the principles by which it works so well for these people could work as well for families with a child or adult member who is mentally retarded, or families with an elderly member who is physically fit but mentally frail. And, as we shall see in the chapter on housing, its approach could be taken further still.

What Crossroads and the other schemes sketched here do is to start from where families are and to offer them the help to live there more fully. They reject the notion that families must be 'wonderful' – and so cope unaided with the gaps between their needs and their resources. They reject too the notion that families must inevitably be 'sad', their 'tragedy' only to be relieved by removal of the person with a disability. They offer families the space to get on with their everyday lives and the support to do so in their own way. And in doing that, they offer people with a disability a stronger springboard for their own everyday contacts with the outside world. The next chapters look at what they may meet there.

4

Making Contact

Laura Brown had, she reckons, a pretty 'normal' childhood. She went to a local school, she enjoyed and scrapped with her brothers, she had the kind of parents who believed in emphasizing what their children could do, rather than what they couldn't. She got herself a higher education and a professional training. She has a good job and enough money to run her own house and large garden. She counts herself lucky to have grown up with the sort of attitudes instilled by her upbringing and to have had the opportunities she's met along the way. The fact that polio at the age of five left her with weakness in her legs, and generally less strong than she looks, hasn't dragged her down; she copes — and she clearly copes pretty well.

But there's another side to her life, too. 'The bit I really don't want people to know about', she says:

> is the cost to myself of coping, and I know I play this down. Part of the difficulty is that very mundane chores take so long and are ridiculously exhausting. Each thing in itself is so trivial that it isn't really worth mentioning, but to try to convey the gist of it: when I put clean sheets on the bed, it probably takes me half an hour as I have to rest during it and finish up fairly exhausted; when I've done a supermarket shop — where, bless them, they put the bags in the car for me — I have to decant the bags into smaller quantities and make six or eight journeys into the house . . . I'm not very good at asking for help, and I know I sometimes worry people, such as neighbours, who fear that I won't ask when I need it.

She reflects sometimes on whether that 'normal' upbringing was altogether an unmixed blessing.

The profound drawback only caught up with me later — that I wasn't as 'normal' as everyone had gone to such lengths to prove I was, but that I had very little equipment for coping with the differences that were impinging on me. The underlying reason, it seems to me now, is that if all the 'positives' are emphasized, there is really no 'space' allowed for recognizing the frustration, the sense of missing out and the anger of *not* being able to do some things. I often suspected, but could never say, that in being praised for achievement there was the unspoken tag 'considering she's disabled'. As a result, I've never really felt sure what things I am any good at. Yet perhaps I am trying to convince myself that if I hadn't been disabled I wouldn't have been the self-driving, competitive person that I am, having to do more than most people to convince myself that I am average. How far have I tended to use the fact of being disabled as a convenient peg on which to hang all my faults and failings — almost as if I had a phantasy of an ideal me which wasn't disabled and, by implication, wouldn't be tormented by my lack of confidence, self-hatred, doubts about sexual relationships, etc.? These things have taken years to work through and still rear their ugly heads at intervals.

Making contact with others could, she knows, be easier if she were an extrovert instead of the introvert she is. But it could be easier, too, if she didn't run into attitudes from those others which are patronizing and devaluing, if the fact of her disability didn't seem to throw barriers in the way of relationships which go beyond the simply formal. She doesn't, by any means, meet those attitudes from everyone she meets. But if a disability is visible, she reckons, it's bound to affect other people and they will react according to their own notions of what disability means. 'I often think it is not only the first, but the only thing that is noticed about me in these casual passings. The thing that seems to be so difficult is to be inconspicuous, ordinary, just one of the crowd. I would love to have normal anonymity which doesn't devalue but also isn't even noticed.' The barriers to relationship aren't always there, either. But they can be often enough for her to have discovered that it can be a great help, when meeting an unknown group of people, to have with her a friend who 'treats me as a normal person — i.e. human — and thereby offers a kind of bridge by which other people can see me as someone worth relating to'. There are enough people in her life who patronize her, enough people who don't seem to find her really human, to leave her with a large question:

Who am I? Do I belong in the able-bodied or disabled society? I find I sit on so many boundaries, and fences aren't very comfortable. My prime reference group is the able-bodied, where I work, have my friends, which is the way I think. And yet I'm not really part of it, because some parts of it won't have me as an equal member.

Not all of us would have Laura Brown's perception of 'two societies' or her question about which we belong to, whether we count ourselves as having a disability or not. As another woman, who does, says: 'Disabled people, as much as anyone else, *are* society. Society is made up of the short and the tall, the bright and the dim, the calm and the volatile, the able-bodied and disabled. My place in society concerns me not at all until someone threatens it by deeming it necessary to define it.' People who have grown up with a disability may find themselves reacting differently to the perception than people who have acquired one in later life, when their friendships have been made and their patterns of living and working established.

But nevertheless, many of us might find an echo of that perception — in the apparent gap between our 'two societies' of work and home, where we may seem to ourselves to be different people, or in the curious fact that two sets of friends, who after all have us in common, simply don't have anything to say to each other. Where does the 'real me' belong? We might wonder what drives us, what we are trying to prove; we might wonder if there isn't an unspoken tag — 'considering he's black, considering she's a woman' — attached to approval for our actions. There are echoes, too, of her experience.

43

There can't be many of us who don't remember moments when instant anonymity would have been better than the embarrassment of standing out in the crowd. There can't be many of us, either, who don't in one way or another regulate how we appear and act by the unspoken agreements of our society on the range of behaviour that is acceptable to it.

For a start, most of us will introduce ourselves in a way that establishes at least some similarity between ourselves and those we meet, rather than by instantly pointing out the differences; that is what making contact is about. So, for instance, a woman who is deaf never pretends that she can hear, 'but if I am likely to come into contact with strangers, I have found that the best approach is to talk and give myself a chance to lipread and answer, so they see that I will understand them, and then tell them and explain.' So a girl with an artificial leg says: 'I always try to get talking to someone before I tell them or they find out.' We have all grown up with a series of patters to ease the uncertainties of first encounters and most of us trot them out every day of our lives. So, for instance, a young man who is mentally retarded has painstakingly learned the patters of his own family circle, and will enquire politely after the health, the journey, the family, of those he meets. As meetings turn into the beginnings of relationships, things may sometimes get a bit harder. We may find ourselves having to bluff it, to pretend, for the sake of maintaining contact, that we understand more than we do. So, for instance, another young man who is mentally retarded has perfected the bluff that hides his inability to tell the time: he glances at his watch, at the activities going on around him and comes up with answers like 'Nearly lunchtime', which he knows will satisfy most of the people most of the time. Sometimes we will find ourselves in situations where, for the sake of what we hope to gain, we not only put up with people we dislike, but go to some lengths to pretend we enjoy their company. One woman who has a severe disability, for instance, finds relationships a great strain.

One must not show one's feelings of irritation, envy and boredom, in case one loses a useful source of help. No doubt you have noticed that many disabled people are always cheerful, smiling and joking. This is because they know it is the only way to get people to help them. Among themselves, they behave normally, but before others, they put on an act to soothe the guilty feelings of those they hope to use.

As we go about making contact, we will not only try, to one degree or another, to 'fit' with those we meet. We will take with us an image of the way we want to be seen. We may choose to present ourselves as competent, self-reliant, however much it may cost us physically or emotionally. A woman who went to a special school for blind girls, for instance, remembers:

> We were really harsh with anyone who showed us up. If a group of girls from another school came to visit and one of us dropped her teacup, or knocked something over, they would be almost punished for it by us later — at least, they would be really humiliated by our jokes and imitations of them and their mistakes.

She still feels, especially at work, that she must be seen to be coping better than anyone else.

> I feel I have to be really good, on time, not ill often and always producing my best. I don't want to give anyone the chance to criticize me, or think I cannot cope because of being blind. It can be quite exhausting. I try to present this "I'm very balanced, normal and capable" front to colleagues. I know it's probably unnecessary, but I find it difficult to lower those standards I've set myself now.

Others among us may take a completely opposite tack. We may reject entirely any notion of 'fit', but instead choose to stand out from the crowd by the way we dress, speak and the views we hold. We may choose from the start to emphasize what makes us different, and if we don't make contact as a result, then that's because these are people we don't want to make contact with. Or we may use the differences to get what we wanted in the first place. We all know people, usually not ourselves, who will play down their abilities to get others to organize the party ('You've all got so much imagination, I only wish I had') or do some chore ('I'd love to help but I'm overwhelmed with work'). So people with disabilities will sometimes know someone − usually not themselves − who uses the differences in the same way:

> Some disabled people seem positively to enjoy it. From being a woman who looked after her family and nobody bothered about very much, she is now the centre of attention. She is usually very fat and sits in her wheelchair like a hen on a nest. She needs at least three men to lift her and insists that it isn't any use trying to slim.

We all know people who enjoy being helpless.

Wherever we stand on the spectrum, most of us will probably have moments of sensing the gap between the 'real me' and the one that we present to the world. Some people perhaps won't; they will never, in their whole life, for one instant, have dissembled, or concealed a flash of feeling, or tailored themselves to their surroundings. But then they probably won't be reading this book, for they will have hit perfection. The rest of us will perhaps find some echo in A.H. Sutton's recollection of growing up with severe cerebral palsy:

> For as long as I can remember, I have been conscious of two 'mes' − the outer casing which is visible to the world and the inner substance which is not. The outer casing is, of course, my body, and it is the façade by which, in all but a few circumstances, the world judges me. The inner part is my mind, my character, my conscience, my true being. So it is, of course, with everybody . . . but . . . the fact is that my life has been a constant conflict involving these two parts. Even [as a child] I was conscious of my body and my appearance. Kids used to come up to me and ask what my name was, didn't I know it? What time was it? Why couldn't I talk properly, why was I shaking? It didn't take long for me to appreciate the situation, yet I knew the answers to their questions . . . In my early teens, this

46

problem of appearance became worse. I became very self-conscious and this in turn made my speech, already poor, worse still. My father, a successful businessman, had friends to whom he introduced me, but I could never say anything which they could interpret and I could see their growing embarrassment, sometimes writing me off as imbecilic. I had at these times to retain a very firm grasp of my inner being to avoid − to avoid what? I don't know − possibly insanity.

There is nothing 'different' in the range of tactics that people with disabilities use to make contact with others; they are all perfectly 'normal'. What is different is what happens if the tactic misfires. Most people, if they don't make the first impression they choose to, usually get the chance to recoup; people with disabilities may not, they may find that they are 'typed' and lose their chance to be seen as themselves. The woman who is deaf knows that well-intentioned friends who rush in with the information before she has had the chance to make her own contact, do her a great disservice: people will ignore her, talk over her; they are 'put off'. The girl with an artificial leg knows that if people learn about this before she has made contact, she meets all sorts of reactions she neither seeks nor needs: 'people are either adament that they don't want to get involved with me in any way, or go to the other extreme and are over-curious and somewhat over-protective, which is, needless to say, maddening.' The young men who are mentally retarded know far too well the consequences of failing to establish their contact with the 'normal' world − the large and small rejections, the assumptions that limited understanding means no understanding at all and no ordinary feelings, either. The woman who is blind knows that she has to fight all sorts of assumptions about the inability of 'people like her' to cope. So, for instance, she will wash her clothes if there is the slightest chance that they might be dirty: 'I feel that I daren't look tatty or have any stains on my shirt, because people will think it's "because I'm blind"; they won't ever assume that I chose to be tatty or scruffy'.

The first difference, then, is in the reactions that people

with disabilities meet in their contacts with a world in which the majority do not share them. The second difference is that people with disabilities may have fewer alternatives if the contact fails to give them the chance to be seen for themselves rather than those disabilities. Most people can afford to miss a few chances for contact, because others will come up; people with disabilities may find they get the same reactions over and over again. Most people can choose how much of the 'inner me' they bring out from behind the façade and may spend a fair amount of energy perfecting the façade to protect it. People with visible disabilities may spend far more time trying to persuade people that the façade isn't the 'real me' at all, but with less choice in the matter, because the façade is what brings the reactions, and explaining that appearances aren't everything can be hard. 'People call me "Are you a mongol?"' says one woman; 'I am not. "Are you a handicap?" I am not. But I'm just on the border, on the edge of it, I am.'

There is nothing to say that the barriers are inevitable. Countless people with disabilities and their friends and acquaintances could show that they most certainly are not. But they are there between enough people enough of the time not to be glossed over. The world makes its judgements on appearances and immediate impressions; it uses these to bolster all sorts of assumptions that have little to do with the truth. And in doing so, it makes for handicaps not just among people who have disabilities, but among people who would say that they do not.

'To be a child stammerer', says one man who now gets by pretty well as an adult one, 'is a bit like being invisible; no one ever asks you any questions, and I was at university before I was expected or even encouraged to participate in discussions. Yet like the person who is small and feels big I don't feel like a stammerer. With my looks, wit and intelligence, I feel like a star . . .' Yet others meet him with embarrassment or worse.

As soon as a stammerer begins to ply his trade, some people try to help by finishing words which he was not going to say in the first place; others look at him as though he's a bit barmy and either try humouring him in case he should happen to be carrying an axe in his raincoat pocket, or speak in a VERY LOUD VOICE, imagining him to be also afflicted with deafness.[1]

If people who *are* deaf met more who simply spoke up when they met them, they might find making contact a lot easier than they often do. 'No affliction generates so much ridicule, contempt and confusion as a deaf person among "normals".' The man who said that has had his chances to make comparisons, as he has also been partially-sighted since he was born and now has difficulty in walking as well. People who are deaf, it seems to him, are thought to be 'daft' and generally unreliable − or simply rude and not attending to what's being said. The possibility that they just can't hear doesn't seem to be considered.

This is particularly true before the deaf person 'comes out' and explains − but it is not always appropriate during some types of social interaction ever to get to the stage of explaining the deafness. These sorts of casual meetings and encounters can be really traumatic for the deaf person, for they tend to undermine confidence in oneself, eat away at self-esteem and call for either withdrawal from meeting people, or a more aggressive stance such as 'Well, I don't give a damn *what* they think of me, I shall go right ahead anyway.' So, in essence, it's this business of always having to explain oneself, as if continually apologizing for one's existence, that makes it so hard.

Far easier, he feels, to have a disability that people can *see*: 'People are tolerant, helpful and generally sympathetic to my bad leg when they see exactly what the difficulties are. "Normals" can assess and cope with tangible practicalities much better than the mental and emotional ambiguities of sensory handicaps.'

But can they always? A woman who has severe arthritis finds that people talk to her 'as though I was simple.' The girl with an artificial leg finds: 'Many people feel entitled to know everything about my disability and feel genuinely indignant when I decline to fill them in; many don't know where to draw the line, so some remarks really hurt.' The world draws its conclusions and they are not always generous. So a woman is staggering down the street, grasping for support. Her problem is that she has a trapped nerve in her spine. But what the neighbours cluck as they watch her creep towards her door is: 'Drunk — and at this hour of the morning!' A man who had spells, over ten years, of staggering, impaired vision, muscular spasms, incontinence and fatigue got very tired of being dismissed as drunk when he, in fact, had multiple sclerosis. Now he is in a wheelchair, he finds attitudes are quite different; even when he has indeed had one too many, he finds people kind and generous. A woman who all her life has had difficulty in walking underlines his point: 'Better, for a woman, to look all romantic in a wheelchair than to stagger round in an ungainly fashion!'

But some people who go about in wheelchairs may see things differently, for they may find that their very obvious inability to walk brings assumptions of all sorts of other inabilities as well. The very design of their transport, after all, ensures that any conversation held by someone pushing them is quite literally over their head. Young people can find out early on what they have to contend with. A group of them remembered a visit to a fair together, where they were all given prizes, whether they had won them or not: that took all the fun away, they reckoned, as well as being bad for the fairground's business. They remembered being offered icecreams by complete strangers at the seaside. A boy remembered his infuriation at being 'allowed' to win at table-tennis by an able-bodied opponent. 'When mum takes me out,' says a young girl, 'I find people are very strange towards me. They look at me in a very funny way. They think I am mad, just because I am in a wheelchair. When mum is pushing me, old people stop us, and they say to mum: "What a lovely girl you have!" This I can't stand. Why can't they speak to me?'

It's a question that many of her elders — and not just those in wheelchairs — might echo. Not for nothing is a current English wireless programme for people with disabilities called 'Does He Take Sugar?'. But wheelchairs can carry a very clear message, and a woman who tackles her busy job in health administration from one knows what it can be like at the receiving end.

> Following an extremely traumatic morning — picking up members, visiting the maternity unit, car breaking down, no time for lunch — I arrived at the nurses' prizegiving, breathing a sigh of relief that I'd managed to collect yet another load of members and get them there on time. A reverend gentleman appeared. 'How nice,' he says, 'that they managed to bring you along!' How that guy is still alive I'll never know!

Adolescence can bring its own problems:

> One's teenage years are normally one's worst, and with me it was no exception. I think the complete realization of my hopeless situation, or so it seemed, came when I saw boys of my own age walking out with girls. Sex had suddenly assumed an importance and a new significance. The first sexual urges I experienced brought with them probably the culmination of the conflict . . . which sprang out of the knowledge that mentally I was alert, but physically repulsive. I sat in my room alone and despaired.

A.H. Sutton, like most adolescents, came out from his sense of isolation; we have glimpsed his 'normal' marriage. But if the barriers that people with disabilities run into as they go about making sexual and emotional contact have their echoes in most 'normal' experience, their intensity can seem to accentuate 'difference'.

People will have their own doubts about their attractiveness. One woman remembers how desperately afraid she and the others at her special school for blind girls were that no 'normal' man would look at them — and the sense that there would be something wrong with him if he did. She is now married to a sighted man, but she knows others who feel she is 'not quite a woman'. A woman who is severely paralysed reckons to meet three kinds of response from men. Complete rejection is the first: 'If I don't like their remarks, I answer back in kind:

there've been a few feet I've run over with my wheelchair, too'. The second is over-enthusiasm, fuelled by drink or the attention that comes for a 'predicament' rather than a person, and only ever a temporary ego-boost. The third is admiration, which can bring its quota of older men, usually with hard-luck stories about their wives and other problems, and 'religious salesmen'.[2] The old sexual stereotypes which lay down tougher standards for women's appearance than they do for men's may be at work. One woman, for instance is used — because she has to be — to the flicker of interest that disappears when she starts to walk crookedly. A man who has far more obvious a disability in his legs than she may, after years, still hesitate to appear on the beach in swimming trunks; but he also knows that he's been characterized as having 'an interesting limp', and he doesn't reckon that it has spoiled his chances.

Building on first contacts may bring an intensification of very 'normal' problems. People who live with their parents, may have to contend with the protectiveness that comes with concern about exploitation; people who are mentally retarded in particular may find their parents unwilling to take their friendships and aspirations seriously. There may be the normal problem of privacy — but intensified, because disability may mean that you simply can't leap quickly into your clothes. There may be particular barriers, too. 'How will he react to a mature individual who wears plastic knickers and pads and requires help when going to the loo? Rejection on this count can be very grim and frustrating.'[3]

The world can throw up its own barriers too. One woman had to get used to the neighbours referring to her husband as 'that gentleman we've seen you with': the notion that a nice girl like her would get involved with a physical mess like him was clearly too much altogether, particularly as it brought its own queries about what he, in his obvious violation of the norms of masculinity, had that others hadn't. Another woman is tired of insinuations that there is something 'odd' about her able-bodied partner; she is tired of the sexual stereotyping that says 'normal' men don't take on a caring role.

For others, the world's reactions may be borne out. One woman has not found making contact either easy or satisfying since her marriage ended, because, she reckons, her husband couldn't stand having a wife with a disability. 'That's how I know there is no God. If there were, he would not have made me a sexual animal.' A man who, like her, grew up with a difficulty in walking, has known what involuntary abstinence is like since his wife divorced him. 'It's bad enough when there is a taboo on sex, but with the handicapped this is doubly so and I feel this quite a lot. Usually I settle for "creative" outlets like writing. This is possibly restricting, preventing normal development.'

For some people, at whatever age, disability can bring a more general loneliness. A woman who lives alone, for instance, and has had an intense and undiagnosed pain in her limbs for over ten years, says that she sees no one unless she goes to Mass, which she tries to do every day. Her brother and sister have no notion, she says, of what it is like to feel ill most of the time. She feels very very lonely. Her day usually starts at about four a.m.; she has lunch at about eleven. 'The day seems terribly long, and I am tempted to eat, merely for something to do.' But the experience can also be the very opposite: 'The word "lonely" so often used when talking of disabled or elderly people, makes me want to scream. I probably see more people now than I ever did before, and dread being grabbed by women who jabber endlessly at you because you cannot escape by moving away.' Neither of these women has found it possible to make the sort of contact they want.

At the limit, the reactions that people meet in their search for this contact can lead to what Judith Thunem has called 'the invalid mind'. She writes from the perspective of someone who grew up with a disability, but what she has to say could apply more widely.

Since the person disabled early in life is nearly always treated as an inferior, he develops a strong feeling of inferiority. Being often humiliated, he naturally seeks to avoid humiliation. He tends to become suspicious and sensitive, feeling snubs where none are intended. He lacks self-respect, and often suffers rather than take the trouble of trying to fight back. He doesn't complain, because he is afraid of being

53

accused of self-pity. He shows humbleness and thankfulness because he finds such behaviour serves him well, not because he feels any real thankfulness or friendliness towards the gracious benefactor or, perhaps more often, benefactress. He often hides his bitterness behind a smiling face, and secretly despises the normal world which is so easily deceived and taken in. He firmly believes that normal people neither can, nor will, understand his troubles. This way of thinking is the natural result and outcome of his experiences. But nevertheless, it is a dangerous state of mind. A person brooding on wrongs done to him isn't easy to get into contact with. His distorted mind colours everything done to him by normal people. Even when treated with respect he senses an intolerable and condescending attitude. So the contact seekers from the other side of the wall have a hard time of it trying to break through.

That is not a description of people with a disability; it is a description of a handicap. And that handicap is a mutual one. Paul Williams is writing on behalf of people who are severely mentally retarded, but others may find something in what he says:

When one of us meets one of you, especially if it is for the first time, we are quite likely to lack many of the skills for successful communication. We may not be able to think of anything appropriate to say, or to put it into the right words, or to control our facial expression. But you also will show a great lack of skill. You will be embarrassed, you won't be able to think of anything appropriate to say, you will tend to talk in an inappropriate tone of voice, you will tend to have a wide grin on your face and ask questions without really being interested in the answer. The handicap is thus a mutual one. Both of us have difficulty in communicating with and forming relationships with the other. The trouble is that you have lots of opportunity to go off and form relationships more easily. We don't. You can deny your handicap. We can't – we live with it all the time . . .

We've got few hang-ups about talking to you or sharing

things with you or touching you, because we do not see you as very different from ourselves. It doesn't particularly worry us when you can't think what to say to us, when you can't control your facial expression, when you're embarrassed in our company. We share these handicaps with you. The difference is that it hurts us when you turn away, but it relieves you when we turn away. In that lies our strength and your need.

If disabilities must be lived with, handicaps can be alleviated. So what to do?

The usual first answer has to do with 'changing attitudes' and 'public education'. But the trouble with campaigns to change attitudes is that, like exhortations to love our neighbour, they usually touch only the converted, and the person we meet may be one of the others. The trouble with 'public education' is that most of us take the public to mean the other person, and go on making our private contacts in the way we have always done. Maybe it's time to look instead to changing some of our behaviours and to some very individual education.

'When I first became disabled,' says one elderly man:

one of the things I noticed and silently resented was the efforts of well-meaning neighbours not to allow me to do anything. On one occasion I was using a hammer and saw in the garden when one of these individuals came rushing up. He literally snatched the tools from my hands and proceeded to do this little job that was well within my capacities, and I had to watch him, trying not to look futile, while he cut himself with the saw and hit himself with the hammer. When he went away, bloody but quite obviously pleased with himself, I set about the job and did it to my satisfaction. Now I'm glad to say that all my friends and relatives leave me alone, knowing that if I need assistance I won't be in the least reluctant to ask.

There is nothing 'normal' at all about the inability to do ordinary 'normal' things that a physical disability brings with it, and the confusion that this generates is at the heart of the

55

mutual handicap. Small children escape the confusion: they haven't yet learned what the 'norms' of capability are. But adults know perfectly well that it is not 'normal' to need individual help to get about, to keep your house in reasonable working order. The fact that we are all dependent on a host of others to sustain our daily lives doesn't take away the difference in degree when that help may boil down to help with getting to the lavatory. And whether we have a disability or not, that difference in degree can present us all with problems.

Appearing independent and capable, as we have seen, is central for some people with disabilities; they reckon it to be the essential of leading 'as normal a life as possible' and they may, like Laura Brown and the woman who is blind, make considerable investments of time and energy to meet the world's standards. Asking for help can be difficult for anyone who is trying to underline the similarities between themselves and others rather than the differences. A woman who put in for a handrail at the steps leading to her office was told to ask people to help her up and down instead. 'It's not that people are unwilling, but no one seems to understand how soul-destroying it is to keep asking for help all the time.'

The reluctance to ask for help can bring its problems. One woman, who grew up with a tubercular hip, remembers how she, with a full-time job and two children, felt she must keep a spotless house, to counteract the feeling of her (mostly non-working) neighbours that a woman with a disability had no business having children at all. 'No quarter given or help offered – and how senselessly I worked myself into the ground.' She still is determined to be seen as capable and she is, too. But she also feels saddened at the lack of offers of help, and frustrated at the lack of understanding of the extra effort she has to put in to achieve her 'normal' life.

Some people are in a different situation: they can't get by without help. But that can bring its problems too. 'The bit about being helped that really gets me', says Laura Brown:

is when someone offers to do something but doesn't ask how I want it done. I'm not terribly obsessional, but there are some things which I have got very carefully organized in a special way so that they are manageable. The helper can't know this, I know, but if he or she bulldozes a different system of height, place, order, I may be sunk and have endless problems in trying to undo what they did in their attempts to be helpful.

A man with multiple sclerosis talks of the 'utter frustration of being physically incapable of doing something which one knows perfectly well how to do and having to explain it to somebody else who often thinks he or she knows a better way of doing it and does it that way'. The woman who is blind finds that some people

> get very angry if you say, 'Do you mind not holding me round the waist, it makes things a bit difficult,' or 'Actually, it's easier if I don't hold on to you while I'm going down steps.' They get rather huffy and say 'I'm only trying to help, dear,' and stalk off. It's often just their fear and embarrassment, or their shock, maybe, that you actually have ideas of your own.

She understands, better than some, perhaps, that if asking for help can be a problem for people with disabilities, offering it can be a problem for the people they meet. These people too, after all, have learned that 'as normal a life as possible' is what their fellows with disabilities want to lead; they too are embarrassed at underlining the 'abnormality' which a need for help may signify. They are handicapped in their understanding of when 'help' is helpful and when it hinders — and if people with disabilities may seem reluctant to explain for fear of appearing too demanding, those who are trying to 'help' may be just as reluctant to emphasize the 'abnormality' by asking for explanations. They too can only take people at face value. Are they supposed to guess that someone who appears capable and energetic is secretly wishing for help all the time? Are they supposed to guess where people want things put if there is no indication from them that there is an order which is important?

It is a mutual handicap which can only be dented by education and that means a willingness to teach on one hand

and a willingness to learn on the other. And that in turn means, perhaps, a re-think of the values of 'independence'. For some people with disabilities, 'independence' means not coping alone, but choosing whether to do so or not, choosing whether to put their energy into getting on with everyday life, or to accept more help there so that they have more energy left for other things. The point is not that one choice or another is 'better' but that both are equally valid. To get to this point, we have all perhaps to remember just how interdependent we in fact are in our complex societies, and to widen the boundaries of this 'normality'. We have all, perhaps, to get a bit nearer the sorts of relationships with those we meet that can admit to inabilities rather than hide them. It's a tall order. But we won't even begin unless the people who perhaps have most to teach and those who have perhaps the most to learn can get together. That is what the next chapter is about.

5

Getting Together

A woman decides to go to an art exhibition. She can't exactly drop everything and go while she's in the mood; preparations for going out take some time, and so does phoning around a number of friends to find one who is free and wants to see the exhibition too. Once she arrives there, she can't exactly just go in. Her friend has to find an official and he has to find his friend and between them all, she manages to get out of her wheelchair, into the hoist, see her chair safely up the stairs and get back into it again. She and her friend are directed to the special entrance to the exhibition itself. The first thing they see when they go in is a sign saying 'The End'. They spend some time trying to see if they can't, like everyone else, visit the exhibition in sequence. They find out that it would be so complicated to do so that they give up and see it backwards and sideways instead. The woman in the wheelchair ends up with a crick in her neck from straining upwards at pictures above her eye-level throughout. Then they go through the whole business of the hoist again and as people pause to watch, she feels as if she's on exhibition herself. By the time she gets home, she remembers almost less about the exhibition than about the hassle of getting there and back, and she's too tired to do anything except go to bed. She wonders whether it was worth it.

A young man decides to go to the local pub. He's been there once or twice already, though never alone. There's a jostle at the bar and it's some time before he's served; other people push ahead of him; they don't seem to have learned about taking your turn. The bar is very noisy — perhaps that's what ails the barman, for he is rather rude and sighs impatiently while the young man decides what to drink, and he seems to have trouble understanding the order. When the young man offers to pay with a note, the barman is cross and seems to have trouble finding the change. When eventually the drinker makes his way to a free seat, the other people at the table don't seem very friendly; he finds that they aren't very good at talking to strangers. He finishes his drink and leaves. The next time someone suggests he goes to the pub, he says he'd rather settle for an evening in front of the television.

Most of us will know moments when we have had to think carefully about our relationship with our physical environment — even if it is only as we negotiate slippery stones across a stream. A broken leg, or arm, a hurt back, are reminders enough of how much we generally take that environment for granted. Most of us will know flashes of frustration at the conspiracy of inanimate objects to get between us and what we are trying to do. Most of us will have moments of confusion when we haven't mastered the rules in one social setting or another. The relationships that people with disabilities can have with the different environments they find themselves in may not be very different in kind. But they can be very different indeed in degree.

'What I feel the able-bodied person does not realize', says one woman who gets about in a wheelchair:

is the tremendous self-discipline the disabled life entails. The able-bodied are confined by duties to family, work and society, but beyond that can do what they want. Society is structured to make it easy for them. They can travel when and where they want to, come and go as they please, often without realizing how easy it is. But for the disabled practically nothing can happen when you want it to. Travel is limited, shopping difficult or impossible, entertainment has to be planned like a campaign. You can do nothing spontaneously. If you want to go out with friends to the pub, for instance — can you park? Are there steps? Is there a downstairs loo? Because of these restrictions, many disabled give up the unequal struggle and stay at home always.

And for people who are mentally retarded, there may be something of the same deliberate relationship with the environment, if for different reasons. It can take a long time to master the skills we all need in different situations, and a great deal of encouragement not to give up on the effort.

But just how handicapping the limitations imposed by disability become depends either on how well the environment is adapted to the range of abilities of the people who use it, or on the opportunities they have had to learn to cope with it, or both. The fact that the woman at the art exhibition was in a wheelchair obviously had nothing whatever to do with her potential enjoyment of it; she was handicapped by an environment that threw up barriers she could only cross by drawing unwelcome attention to herself and getting worn out in the process. The fact that the young man in the pub was mentally retarded had nothing to do with his potential enjoyment of it. But the fact that he hadn't mastered the skills of keeping a place in the queue, offering the right money for his drink, or approaching strangers in the middle of their own conversation, handicapped him in coping with what sounded to be a less than agreeable bunch of people in the first place. In both cases, the experience was fraught enough to make them wonder if it had been worth it.

For other people in other situations, that question may not even arise. The physical barriers, or those thrown up by their own uncertainty, or both, may be high enough to keep them out altogether. They may find that they are very limited in their choice of places to go and people to meet. 'I wonder', asks one young woman who gets about in a wheelchair, 'if they realize that two steps — just two — is all it takes to keep me from places I might want to go to?'

Instead of a widening of choice, people may find themselves offered a range of compensations for what can get to seem like an 'inevitable' exclusion. So there are special environments — special clubs — and special approaches to ordinary ones — group outings for people who have disabilities. Many people enjoy these very much. Others would wish that they had the chance to enjoy them, like this woman who has had a stroke: 'Although I am a pensioner, I have never been offered a bus outing or a cup of tea, or invited to join a church or given any indication that the community is aware of my existence. I have shed so many tears I don't know how there can be any left.'

But there is nothing to say that people are any more 'club-bable' if they have a disability than if they do not. There is nothing to say, either, that even if they enjoy group activities, they are going to enjoy them with other people just because those other people have a disability too. A young man who went on a special holiday for people with physical disabilities vows never to do it again: 'they didn't want to try anything, do anything'. He wonders why people should assume that his interests have changed just because he has broken his neck; he gets angry at the physical barriers that get between himself and clubs, discos and cinemas. Another man who has cystic fibrosis remembers once ending up in a hospital ward with three other people who had the same disease: 'I found a real sense of being the same as those other people for the first time in my life. So it was good to meet others like me. But I don't think I would want always to go about with other cystics, as this would make us noticeable and self-conscious.' In 'One Body', Audrey Shepherd questions the whole concept of clubs for people with disabilities − from her own perspective as a potential candidate, but an 'unclubbable' one:

> I have been seriously challenged on this point by a young woman, very severely paralysed, who is unable to go out to work. She has no doubt that her life would be much duller and emptier were it not for the [club] and I am sure that she would be echoed by thousands of people, completely housebound apart from the club and the club's activities. All this I can see and understand, and can appreciate all the voluntary work which goes into the life of such clubs. But is it really a good thing to draw into one place and link together in fellowship those whose bond is their disability?

Other clubs, like those run by the Physically Handicapped and Able-Bodied (PHAB) organization in England, take this point, and bring together young people who have disabilities and those who don't, to share activities which can include adventurous holidays. One man reckons that his 'training' with one such club was what eventually persuaded him to join the world.

> In my teens and twenties, I was terribly self-conscious, afraid to go into pubs and discos, because people might laugh at me — how ridiculous. But I effectively carried on the sheltering and cossetting of home — 'smother love'. A person with a disability really has to be forced into doing things, to learn social skills. I like going out and choosing my friends and I feel quite at ease now, with a group of people. For a time I used to think 'Why on earth should I be the one to talk to this guy?' Eventually the penny dropped that I'm in the minority group and the barriers are probably of our own making.

For one young girl, however, the approach of a similiar club isn't what she wants: 'They think', she says bluntly, 'that we're freaks.'

However much people enjoy their special clubs, these are no more a substitute for a wide range of social contacts and choices than they would be for anyone. Many people who are mentally retarded, for instance, would like a wider network of friends than they meet at the club and more opportunities to do things with one or two people instead of so often in a group: 'You don't like to be with the same ones all the time, do you?' Many people who have physical disabilities are tired of the restrictions to their free movement that environmental barriers throw up, whether they are special club members or not.

The questions are not just for the people who must live with them most closely. They are for all of us. For as long as people with disabilities find it hard, or even impossible, to share in an ordinary range of social activities, as long as it remains 'unusual' for them to make their way into pubs, clubs and other places where people meet to enjoy mutual interests, the mutual handicap that lies between them and the majority will be reinforced. For as long as their only access is in groups, rather than as individuals, there will be a response that says they should come on a 'special' day, at a 'special' time rather than when they freely choose, and another that finds it hard to break through the superficial 'difference' to find the common ground between individuals. What to do?

The barriers that the environment can throw up against people with disabilities — particularly the minority who use wheelchairs — are so obvious that it's not surprising that a good deal of attention has been paid to them. At the last count, not far short of twenty countries had legislation on access to buildings used by the public. But the universal snag has been enforcement. Although by the end of the 1970s, there was in principle nationwide acceptance of sophisticated federal building standards in the United States, some States didn't even have inspection arrangements to check what was happening in practice. In Britain, the 1970 Chronically Sick and Disabled Persons Act laid down that, when new buildings for public use are planned, or older ones adapted, these should be made accessible 'in so far as it is in the circumstances both reasonable and practicable'. Reasonable? Practicable? Who's to say? There are no penalties for deciding that adaptations are neither of these things.

So, in Britain, the spirit of this act can still be ignored altogether, and there are notorious examples. The Government celebrated the Queen's Silver Jubilee in 1977 by pressing the theme of access for people with disabilities to social opportunities. A committee sat, competitions were launched, reports were collated. But when the poster announcing the public exhibition of the gifts the Queen had received was put up, it bore the legend 'Wheelchairs, prams, pushchairs and dogs regretfully not admitted'. With all of London to choose from, the organizers of an exhibition, who knew it would be a major attraction to many people from all over the country, decided to stage it in a delightfully historial setting which was anything but accessible. A fuss was understandably made. So if people who could not walk or see happened to read one newspaper on one day only, they learned that they could in fact go to the exhibition. If, that is, they arrived very early, on one of two days only, were willing to be manhandled up the stairs or leave their guidedogs at the bottom, and if they were through the exhibition and out within three-quarters of an hour.

If some people simply don't think, others think in strange ways. There is the special hostel at one British university for students with disabilities; but half its accommodation is inaccessible to those who get about in wheelchairs because it is on an upper floor and they can't reach it. Students at an American university who happen to be in wheelchairs will find an echo of their own experience: it was only when the special elevator to the student union had been built that it was found to be too small to accommodate an attendant as well as a wheelchair. There are the specially designed lavatories which are large enough to take wheelchairs but not large enough for their occupants to close the door behind them; so they have the embarrassing and quite unnecessary job of asking for help to push the chair back in when they are ready to leave. There are the special lavatories which are at the bottom of a flight of steps and/or locked if you manage to get to them. It isn't only people in wheelchairs who suffer. One elderly man knows how distressing this is for his wife; he wonders whether ramps and easy access to public lavatories are really so difficult to provide. They have found their own solution: they carry a jam jar in the car. 'In 1980! I hope this is not going to be taxed next. To be disabled and bursting to go is not funny.'

There are less dramatic examples than this and people have to cope with them every day. Even a few steps may throw up insuperable barriers to the most ordinary of activities – shopping, going to the bank or post office, visiting friends or the pub. Supermarket doors may be too narrow for wheelchairs, lift buttons may be pitched too high for their occupants. Kerbstones and uneven pavements are a hazard for people who are blind as well. Pedestrian precincts are not always the agreeable experience their planners intended for anyone who cannot walk far without tiring. Regulations compound the problems: hygiene rules in foodshops where blind people cannot take their dogs.

An environment which is totally convenient for all people all the time is probably a dream, if only because different people have different needs; the ramp that offers access to people in wheelchairs may limit it for people who walk with difficulty and find it easier to negotiate steps. But if planners and designers and people who run shops remembered that people who have disabilities are also people who want to use their community like any other member of it, they could do a whole lot more than they do now to ensure that they can. They might realize, like the designer of a highly accessible and convenient shopping centre in the North of England, that what works for many elderly people and mothers with prams can work also for others who have disabilities; he had not even thought that they might want to go shopping until the advantages of his design were pointed out to him. They might look at some of the research in the United States which suggests that to make a new building completely accessible adds only half of one per cent to the total cost. They might remember that making places inaccessible doesn't just handicap people with disabilities, but handicaps everyone.

Work on access assumes that people can get where they want to go in the first place. But buses are only accessible to people who can negotiate the steps to them and often quickly at that. A woman with a heavy limp as an aftermath of polio finds she is not one of them. 'Why are they so nasty? They should help, shouldn't they?' She wonders if her problems stem from the fact that she spent many years in a mental institution, where she never used a bus at all. An elderly woman with arthritis who has been told by hurried passengers that 'people like her' shouldn't be using public transport at all, could tell her that they don't, and thousands of people could confirm it. For disabled Londoners, there are now reserved seats on the underground − something that the Paris Metro has been offering people disabled in the war for some years − but you still have to be able to get to them. And for most people in wheelchairs who want to travel by rail, it's still most usually an unheated guard's van, together with the racing pigeons and luggage, with no thought at all for an accessible lavatory.

Thought is beginning to go into public transport. By 1980, a few British trains were accessible to wheelchairs, but only on major routes and only if the journey was booked well in advance. The new Tyne and Wear· metro in the North of England has been made accessible, at considerable extra cost.

66

But, on the whole, Britain has preferred to enable people whose physical disabilities are severe to opt out of the public transport system altogether. Yet the mobility allowance, paid to people who are unable or virtually unable to walk, is not pitched high enough to guarantee anything like normal freedom of movement in taxis. People whose disabilities used to qualify them for a Government-issue 'invalid car' no longer have this option, as no new invalid cars have been issued since the beginning of the 1970s and no comparable, but safer, vehicle has replaced them. Motability, the alternative scheme for leasing adapted cars, or buying them on instalments, is simply too costly for anyone who doesn't have extra income to top up the mobility allowance. At least one group of people have definitely become less mobile during the 1970s, rather than more. Those too young to qualify for a driving licence but who used to qualify for an invalid car instead are now having to rely on the good-will of others to get about — and that at the time of their lives when they might most want to be out and doing with contemporaries. By 1980, a far larger group of people was also facing the prospect of reduced, rather than increased, opportunity to get about. A Government proposal to limit parking concessions to people with the most severe disabilities would, if enacted, mean that others who could walk only with difficulty could simply not get to some of the places they wanted to go to.

The United States is taking a different approach. The Government is mandated to make public transport fully accessible to the estimated thirteen million people who can use the existing system only with considerable difficulty or not at all. By the end of the 1970s, the Amtrak railway system was offering people with severe physical disabilities a lot more than a guard's van (with, it's fair to add, far less complete a coverage of the country than British Rail). Wheelchairs can get into each coach of the new long-distance Amtrak trains; there are accessible lavatories in each coach as well as two specially adapted sleeping compartments; the only real snag seemed to be that, once on the train, no one is allowed to stay in their wheelchair.

In other areas of public transport, though, going for bust

seemed to be the problem. The specially-designed Transbus was, by the end of the 1970s, being ordered by some cities to add to their regular bus fleet. But New York, for instance, had warned that the cost of introducing it would bankrupt the nation; Chicago had pointed out that it would cost more than the standard public transport system it had been running for a hundred years. And certainly the money already spent on other, specific projects gives an idea of the scope of the American ambition and the snags. An additional ten million dollars was spent on making the Bay Area Transit System in San Francisco one of the world's most accessible mass transport systems. But that still didn't solve the problem of how people are going to get from the exit to where they want to go next.

Private transport demands private resources; ordinary public transport which is designed to encompass every need of every individual who has a disability looks like Utopia. The answer may lie in a mid-way position which is 'special' to people with physical disabilities, yet has the financial and other advantages of public transport as well. The notion of 'dial-a-ride' buses, which can be ordered up in advance, works in some cities in the United States. It works in the shape of the Telebus service in Berlin; it works in Sweden, where the Stockholm metro is also accessible. Swedish authorities also operate a system of concessionary fares for people with disabilities that extends to taxis; they can save their chits to take long journeys if they so choose. Hard-line activists could reject such schemes as discriminatory. But for many people in Britain, where the one or two 'dial-a-bus' schemes are very far from amounting to even the beginnings of national public transport provision, they could look like the beginning of opportunity.

Physical access to the places you want to go to and even accessible public transport may not mean much if you don't know how to ride the buses or how to use the places they take you to. If people who are mentally retarded have not learned the complex relationship between shopping, preparing what you have bought and producing a meal you enjoy, the supermarket will be as confusing a place to them as ever it was to anyone who had five minutes flat in which to buy the dinner and can't think what to get. If they haven't learned about

68

handling the multiple choices entailed in turning a given amount of money into goods and services, there will be any amount of barriers between them and free movement about their community. For some people, learning these sorts of things may come very slowly; for some others, choice at this level may not mean much at all. But for many, the opportunity of access can be strictly limited, and they are handicapped by its lack.

Many people who are mentally retarded, as we've seen, would like more chances to make contacts outside the social world of the special club; they would like to be able to go off with one or two friends to a place of their choosing, rather than so often in a large group to a place decided to suit majority tastes — or even sometimes, the convenience of the organizers. There's nothing 'abnormal' about these aspirations. But it will be easier, perhaps, for the people who make the bridge between those who are mentally retarded and their communities to ignore them. It will be easier to pay for the drinks in the pub on other people's behalf than to teach them, individually, to acquire this skill for themselves. It will be easier to work out 'special' arrangements with the shopping centre or swimming bath for a group for access at a 'special' time than it will be to teach more people the skills they need to go on their own. It will be easier to fill up the minibus than to teach people how to use public transport with confidence. It will be easier even to assume that they 'like to be with their own kind', without stopping to think who their own kind are.

But a growing number of people who are mentally retarded are finding out that what's easy isn't necessarily what they always want. The young man who had the chance to go regularly to his local pub with a friend until he learned how to use it, now goes sometimes with that friend, sometimes with another; and sometimes, too, he simply drops in on his own to build on the contacts he has made there. The woman who had a regular weekly date with a friend who helped build her confidence in dealing with shopkeepers now has a whole variety of choices in how to spend her Saturday mornings. The young man who has learned how to use public transport independently has discovered that his city by night offers a choice of cinemas, concerts and theatres which make it even more interesting than the city that he used to see by day in a group. Another, who has been patiently introduced to the local gardening club by a friend who knows that 'his own kind' are, among others, people who enjoy making things grow, is still very withdrawn and even strange in his behaviour. But the other gardeners know what unites them and him as well as what makes them 'different' from each other. Another again knows that 'his own kind' are, among others, people who are interested in bicycles; and the members of the cycling club know too that when it comes to bowling across the country, mending a puncture and messing about with spare parts, they and he have a shared delight. Many people who are mentally retarded would like more chances to make more individual contacts like these. As one woman says: 'You don't like to be domineered too often. We're not kids; we're over twenty-one; we're not stupid; we don't like to be domineered . . . It's not right. People have to have a life of your own.'

Fewer physical barriers, more accessible public transport, more opportunities to learn skills, won't take away the obvious limitations that different disabilities bring. But what they will do is to widen the choices available to people, in where they go and whom they go with and whom they meet when they get there. They go beyond the rhetoric of 'public education' and 'changing attitudes' to dent the mutual handicap in practical ways. For it is when more people with disabilities get more ordinary opportunities in their communities that others will find it 'normal' to share those opportunities with those they discover to be not so 'different' after all.

Improving access has to do with widening the boundaries of the 'normal' environment and giving people the tools to use it as they choose. Exactly the same principles can apply to education, to housing, and to work. But before we look at the experiences that people with disabilities may have in these fundamental areas of everyday living, we need to look at some of the barriers that may get between the principles and their application. That is what the next section is about.

6

Perceptions and Practices

Ring the bells, ring!
Hip, hurrah for the king!
The dunce fell into the pool, oh!
The dunce was going to school, oh!
The groom and the cook
Fished him out with a hook
And he piped his eye like a fool, oh!
Children's Encyclopaedia, London, 1808

Men seldom make passes
At girls who wear glasses.
Dorothy Parker, News Item (1893–1967)

Ginger, you're barmy,
You'll never join the army.
You'll never make a scout
With your shirt hanging out.
Ginger, you're barmy.
Chanted at redheads by children all over England,
1950s

Annie is a friend of mine,
She resembles Frankenstein.
When she does the Irish jig
She reminds me of Porky Pig.
Chanted by children, New York, 1950s

Roses are red
Violets are blue
I saw a fat monkey
And I thought it was you
Chanted by children, London, 1980

The cripple is an object of Christian charity, a socio-medical problem, a stumbling nuisance, and an embarrassment to the girls he falls in love with. He is a vocation for saints, a livelihood for the manufacturers of wheelchairs, a target for busybodies, and a means by which prosperous citizens assuage their consciences. He is at the mercy of overworked doctors and nurses and underworked bureaucrats and social investigators. He is pitied and ignored, helped and patronized, understood and stared at. But he is hardly ever taken seriously as a *man*.

Louis Battye 'The Chatterley Syndrome', *Stigma* 1966

I have joined the company of what I call the grotesques, the creatures I have always thought should not have been allowed to disfigure the earth. I have lost three inches in height at the waist, my hands are deformed and my face and neck are swollen by the drugs. I have to wear a back support that juts out at the top like a hump, so that I look like Humpty Dumpty. I cannot wear most of my clothes, and I don't feel like buying others, as I know I will still be a grotesque.

Personal communication, 1980

The Greeks, according to Erving Goffman, used the word *stigma* to refer to 'bodily signs designed to expose something unusual and bad about the moral status of the signifier. The signs were cut or burned into the body and advertised that the bearer was a slave, a criminal or a traitor — a blemished person, ritually polluted, to be avoided, especially in public places.'

Today, he says, the word is applied more to the disgrace itself than to the bodily evidence of it. There are the 'abominations of the body' — the various physical deformities. There are the 'blemishes of individual character' — those inferred from, say, a criminal record, a history of unemployment or radical political behaviour. There is the 'tribal stigma' — of race, nation or religion. What they do is to reduce the bearers, in the minds of the non-stigmatized, the 'normal', from being 'whole and usual' to being 'tainted and discounted'. They are believed, by definition, to be 'not quite human'; so they are discriminated against and their life chances are reduced. They, for their part, are caught by this definition of themselves, for they too see the world with 'normal' eyes; so they see their stigma as a matter for shame. The central feature of their lives becomes the search for acceptance. Living with a disability becomes 'the management of a spoilt identity'.

This is not easy. Goffman elaborates a whole pattern of behaviour to which stigmatized people must resort in their contact with 'normals', who are themselves made anxious by this confrontation with those they hope to avoid. The stigmatized will try to minimize the evidence of their blemish; they will try to 'pass' as normal by concealing as far as they can the fact that they are blemished at all. They will set themselves the often huge task of mastering areas of activity which are usually felt to be closed to them. In their search for 'acceptance', in fact, they will find themselves resorting to all manner of deceit about who they really are.

The analysis is a powerful one, and it could be used to explain many of the ways in which any of us cope with the demands of each other and of our society. Its implications have been accepted by at least one group of people with disabilities: *Stigma* is the title of a book of autobiographical essays as well as Goffman's thesis. But the trouble with explanations like his is that they seem to confirm the inevitable. It is perhaps too easy to forget the most important question: does it have to be like this?

The original Greek meaning of *stigma*, after all, carried no moral connotations; it meant simply a brand, a spot, or a 'moment', a mathematical point. The first people who were branded or 'stigmatized' were slaves, and for reasons which were wholly practical and not at all moral. They were hardly to be avoided, in public places or elsewhere. In a public place, presumably, they were to be seized and returned to their masters who, far from avoiding them, would use them for all sorts of intimate services. In *Attitudes and Disabled People* Vic Finkelstein uses this perception to attack the whole concept of 'stigma' as doing more to make prejudice against people with disabilities respectable than any other in the last couple of decades. Goffman's interpretation, for him, has

obscured the central fact of the life of people with disabilities
– that they too, like the Greek slaves, are an oppressed group
in their society.

Nor has physical disability always brought the 'reduction
of life chances' that Goffman associates with stigma. In
nineteenth-century England and earlier, physical deformity
could be not a barrier to earning a living, but in the crudest
sense at least, an advantage, if that living was begging. As late
as 1925, the psychologist Cyril Burt was able to write, in his
influential *The Young Delinquent*: 'A pale and haggard coun-
tenance, a loathsome-looking skin complaint, a conspicuous
deformity, like a crippled leg or a crooked spine, may become
a real advantage and a rare advertisement.' Among the professional beggars in some countries today, the limbs of very small
children are still said to be twisted and bound, so that they
will attract higher earnings as they grow up.

In the lives of individuals, a stigma may even, at the limit,
bring more positive advantage than this. Sir Arthur Evans, the
discoverer of the Minoan civilization, was obliged to wear
spectacles, which he did reluctantly, because of his extreme
short sight. Yet it was because of that quirk of eyesight, it's
been reckoned, that he was able to examine in such detail, and
to such stunning effect, the tiny Cretan bead-seals and signets
he discovered, undistracted by the wider surroundings that
simply became a blur when he took his spectacles off.

More obviously, a disability may bring no bar whatsoever
to an individual contribution or the world's perception of its
value. A man who had heart disease, who in his later life had
thirty operations for cancer, who had a prosthesis in place of
part of his upper jaw and palate, who sometimes could not
speak, could hardly swallow and hear only with difficulty,
could be said to have had his disabilities. But the work of
Sigmund Freud is not generally considered to be 'outstanding,
considering that he was disabled'.

There is nothing inevitable, either, in the association of
stigma and moral 'badness'. The association during or after a
war, for instance, can be the very opposite – that the person
with a visible disability has made a considerable sacrifice to
help defend the right. A woman who had polio remembers,

as she slithered and stumbled to work in London during the last war, the kindly people who would rush to help her, saying: 'Oh, you poor dear – was it the bombs that did it?' She felt that she was letting the side down by saying that Hitler had nothing to do with her case. A man who had walked with a severe limp all his life, recalls with some glee being stopped by a stranger during the war, who inquired how he had got his wound. When he learned that the limp pre-dated hostilities, he was utterly confused. 'I'm sorry,' he said, 'I was going to sympathize.'

There are, finally, 'unusual bodily signs' which for a very great number of people are evidence of positive moral goodness. Followers of St Francis of Assissi in the fifteenth century, or of Padre Pio in this one, would find in their stigmata evidence of anything but evil.

Yet while we can question the inevitability of Goffman's analysis of disability and of ways of coping with it, it doesn't do either to underestimate the force of the perceptions which produce these. We are all the inheritors of a deadening weight of notions about what disability signifies. And if there have been times in the past when these coloured our practices and provision more obviously than they do today, they are still there to influence them, perhaps the more damaging for being unconscious and implicit rather than conscious and explicit. The very notion of the 'normal', after all, is one not just of statistical measurement, but of 'rightness' or 'fitness'; we ascribe to and pursue a norm of behaviour and achievement because it is morally 'good'. The very notion of the 'abnormal' must equally carry a meaning of 'badness', and so indeed seem something to avoid, in private lives just as in public places.

Disability is unclean, it is polluting; unwholeness is un-holy. There are ancient prohibitions, for instance, against people with disabilities becoming priests. 'And the Lord said to Moses', it says in Leviticus:

> none of your descendants throughout their generations who has a blemish shall draw near, a man blind or lame, or one who has a mutilated face or a limb too long, or a man who has an injured foot or an injured hand, or a hunchback, or a

dwarf, or a man with a defect in his sight or an itching disease or scabs or crushed testicles . . . He may eat the bread of his God, both of the most holy and of the holy things, but he shall not come near the veil or approach the altar, because he has a blemish, that he may not profane my sanctuaries.

Present practices echo ancient perceptions. It is only recently, for instance, that people with severe mental handicaps have had the opportunity to become full members of the Roman Catholic Church; the theological arguments may be complex, but many people could testify to what has seemed like avoidance to them. The opposition to the estabishment of the first hostel for people with mental handicaps in Tel Aviv, in the mid-1970s, would be recognized by anyone who has tried to ensure their stake in ordinary housing. But if that opposition stemmed from a whole host of unfounded fears, there was nothing logical in the final compromise either: the hostel was accepted by its neighbours, provided that none of the people who lived in it had visible physical disabilities.

Perception may be overlaid by a whole host of practical considerations. But it is still there, at the root of them. There may be all the practical reasons in the world for the 'fitness to teach' test that people who want to go to teacher training colleges in England have to pass. But the fact that people who are blind or often have severe physical disabilities can and do teach successfully should at least raise the question of what 'fitness', in this context, really means. There may be a whole host of bureaucratic complexities to uphold the zoning laws which govern the use of property in so many North American cities; but the result is that people with mental handicaps often end up living in a residential establishment sited at the 'dirty', industrial, end of town. The barriers that these people meet when they try to emigrate to so many of our affluent, Western countries have, to be sure, the sort of economic basis that draws the votes of affluent, Western electorates. But what is at the back of them? It was precisely because this group of people was seen as a pollutant, a malign growth that sapped vital national energy, that each of those societies threw up

76

huge, ugly institutions in which to contain them in the earlier years of this century.

The perception of pollution can still become explicit. People with severe diseases of the skin still have to bear with the general assumption that their condition is catching and the revulsion that comes with it; they will say that they are shunned in general hospital wards. There is the story of the woman who came to share a weekend of relaxation and discussion with some people who have mental handicaps and took to carrying a cup in her handbag, which she produced at meals and coffee-breaks. 'Well,' she explained, 'you never know, do you, where their hands have been?' That was her problem. But many people have to bear the brunt of it. A group of people with mental handicaps would like to be able to make themselves a cup of tea and a snack when they feel like it, to invite friends to drop in to the place they call 'home'. But the refrigerator is kept locked and they have no key. And why? 'Well,' explains the person in charge, 'you never know where their hands have been.'

If disability is unclean, it is also evil. The association is part of our everyday vocabulary: we have a 'bad' leg, we have something 'wrong' with us. The opposite of *mens sana in corpore sano* is 'a twisted mind in a twisted body'. And if we are in danger of forgetting what that means, we have Shakespeare's Richard III to remind us: 'Cheated of feature by dissembling nature/ Deformed, unfinish'd, sent before my time/ Into this breathing world scarce half made up/ And that so lamely and unfashionable/ That dogs bark at me as I halt by them' — determined, since he cannot prove a lover, to prove a villain instead. Martin Luther saw the devil in a profoundly handicapped child; in parts of Africa today, such children are still seen as possessed of evil spirits.

Western societies echo the perception in the still powerful notion that disability is a judgement for wrongdoing, though they talk of 'guilt' rather than 'sin'. A mother recalls the discovery that her daughter had severe limitations: 'You never think anything like that can happen to you. You're shattered . . . You feel a race apart. At the beginning, you think if anyone is saying anything, they're talking about you. You feel it's

77

your fault. You feel it's a judgement.'[1] A woman with severe multiple sclerosis would not be the only one to cry: 'I say to religious people, "Why me, why, what did I do?" Oh God, I know I was no saint, but no one deserves this.'

She, like the rest of us, grew up with the association. If there is an Italian proverb that says: 'The squint-eyed are on all sides accursed,' there is also a children's custom in one part of England that says you must spit on the ground to avert bad luck if you see a woman who is cross-eyed. There is another elsewhere that says you must spit over your little finger if you see someone with a wooden leg. We grow up knowing that you can recognize the villains by their physical deformity. Witches are ugly, Captain Hook in *Peter Pan* was bound to be evil. Blind Pew, the beggar who so terrified Jim Hawkins in *Treasure Island* brought the Black Spot and death; if Jim had had his wits about him, he wouldn't have been deceived for a moment about the villainy of the fast-talking, one-legged Long John Silver. The tradition is alive and well in the United States, too. A 1980 analysis of children's comics found that physical disability and wicked characters went together.

Nor is the association between unusual physical signs and evil simply kids' stuff. It has been used to construct whole theories of criminality. In Greek and Roman plays, the inferior person was often played by an actor wearing a red wig, while later Judas Iscariot was often painted with a red beard. While Sherlock Holmes found the cracking of the Red Headed League a one-pipe problem, there is a recent and solemn study of the connection between red hair and banditry in the Wild West. More directly, under some medieval laws, if two people were accused of the same crime, the one who was uglier or more deformed was found guilty.

Ancient perception has become scientific fact. When Cesare Lombroso was a doctor in the Italian Army, he had occasion to do a post-mortem on a famous brigand. It was a revelation. 'At the sight of that skull I seemed to see, all of a sudden, lighted up as a vast plain under a flaming sky, the problem of the nature of the criminal — an atavistic being who reproduces in his person the ferocious instincts of primitive man and the inferior animals.' His *L'Uomo Delinquente*, published in 1876, attracted a huge following. Huge jaws, high cheekbones, odd ears, epilepsy, left-handedness, stammering, bad coordination, large noses, abnormal hairness — all became characteristics of the born criminal. These contentions may seem absurd in this scientifically sophisticated age. But scientific sophistication can serve to perpetuate the perceptions. It only took a report in the mid-1960s on a group of men in mental handicap institutions who had an extra Y chromosome, a criminal record and a resistance to 'conventional forms of correctional training' to raise a public scare that tall men had a chromosome abnormality which was liable to make them dangerous criminals. We know now that an extra Y chromosome is not necessarily associated with mental handicap at all, although it *may* bring an immaturity in development of personality. But then even Lombroso never said that all men with large noses were murderers. It's the association that feeds the perceptions. And the perceptions have their commerical value. The plot of *The Twisted Nerve*, a British film which came out in 1968, rested on the 'fact' that there is a hereditary link between Down's Syndrome and murderous behaviour. After protests from interested organizations, the film was prefaced by a preamble which made it clear that its theme was complete fabrication. But it has since twice been shown on television without the preamble. Twice the company apologized — after the event. And twice, people with Down's Syndrome picked up the damage while the company picked up the ratings.

Perception of disability as evil has led to wholesale and notorious practices. The institutions that sprang up in response to the eugenic scare on both sides of the Atlantic in the early years of this century were not, after all, designed to sweep away only people with mental handicaps, but the whole 'social evil' that had become associated with them. As late as 1929, an influential British report could claim that if all the families with a mentally handicapped member could be gathered together, they would include a much higher proportion than would normally be found of 'insane persons, epileptics, paupers, criminals (especially recidivists), unemployables, habitual slum-dwellers, prostitutes, inebriates and other social ineffectuals'. People still live in those institutions in their thousands.

And if the perceptions that brought an earlier generation to them now seem irrational and even bizarre, those perceptions are still in the very air we all breathe and they must, however unconsciously, influence our practices. Evidence says that people with mental handicaps are less likely to get into trouble with the law than others; yet all over the Western world, petitions are drawn up against their moving into ordinary neighbourhoods, which assert not only that they will drag down property values, but that they will bring danger and violence. Every time people with physical disabilities meet a rebuff – from the refusal of a job to the smallest turning away – the perceptions are a part of the practice. Is there not, after all, something 'wrong' with them?

If people with disabilities have been perceived as unclean, as evil – as embodying everything, in fact, that troubles human beings about the human condition – they have also been separated from the 'whole' by being perceived as not quite human at all. 'It is often hard to believe', says one woman who needs sticks and a wheelchair to get about, 'that one is not a burden to one's family, friends and society. Of course this feeling is kept for the darker hours, but it is real. Just as it is difficult for the able-bodied to believe that the disabled are proper human beings, so is it for the disabled themselves.'

People with disabilities have been seen as qualifying for a place that is little lower than that of the angels. At different times and in different places, they have been revered as specially chosen of God, either for their own attributes or to ward off divine retribution. Blind people have been credited with uncanny and supernatural powers ever since the ancient seers foretold the future. The special position that they have claimed for so long under social welfare legislation and provision may have to do with the instant 'understanding' that their condition evokes, but it carries too this ancient perception; it finds its echo in the fact that the folk-lore of British children still counts it lucky to see a blind man and luckier still to help one.

The sufferings of people with disabilities have been used to point a powerful moral. Children's literature of the nineteenth century is starred with small cripples, shedding light on all around them, showing extraordinary generosity, forgiveness and courage as they meet their premature and beautiful deaths, an example to all. And not just children's literature, either: 'God bless us every one,' cries Tiny Tim, as he convinces Scrooge of the wickedness of his ways. As an attempt to make sense of childhood suffering in a world that knew too much of it — and to remind more fortunate children to be good — these stories may seem clumsy now. But in any country whose traditions are Christian, the suffering that disability may bring must remain a powerful metaphor. In *Blessings*, Mary Craig writes of her severely retarded son: 'If our value as human beings lies in what we do for each other, Paul had done a very great deal; he had, at the very least, opened the eyes of his mother to the suffering that was in the world, and had brought her to understanding something of the redemptive force it was capable of generating.' The truth of the perception, just as the reality of individual suffering, is distorted by practice in our societies, which prefer to put such uncomfortable challenges aside. Practice dictates, as we have seen, that people with disabilities must be either 'wonderful', and so expected to cope unaided, or 'sad', and so to carry pain which is neither inevitable nor their own. In neither case is there room for full humanness.

Nor is there when perception dockets them as 'eternal children', to be protected as helpless, to be shielded from the normal range of responsibilities on that account. Men and women who have mental handicaps know well enough what it can mean to be characterized as 'boys and girls', and it is they who have borne the brunt of this perception. It was only in the 1970s, after all, that the National Association for Retarded Children in the United States and its English counterpart have changed their names — the first to replace 'Children' by 'Citizens' and the second to add 'and Adults' — to explain to the world that the majority of their constituents have left childhood behind them. But the perception is built on every time that the societies concerned with, say, cerebral palsy or arthritis, feature in their advertising an appealing small child rather than the adults who take most of their energy and concern.

The woman with cerebral palsy who joined a day centre

for people with a variety of disabilities knows how this perception translates into practice: 'It was nothing but a kindergarten, do what you're told, or else.' She left. The people on the receiving end of charitable endeavour which assumes that what they most want and need is an 'entertainment', as if they were children to be encouraged by a treat, know too. One man who has been there too often characterizes these events: 'Their whole attitude is "Get them all into mini-vans, lug them off, get them sat down, entertain them – and if ever you're stuck, give them something to eat." ' He is looking for intellectual stimulation, a forum where people can swap notes on coping with their disabilities and learn to live fuller lives. He hasn't found it yet in any of the charitable organizations set up to 'help' people like him.

It was in 1884 that a mental retardation worker characterized one of his charges like this: 'With his great, soft, jet eyes, he reminds one of a seal.' The mental retardation worker who said: 'A lot of them can't talk, the same as animals can't; I've always said that what we need here is a vet, not a psychiatrist,' was talking at the beginning of the 1970s. It is not uncommon to hear the wards of mental institutions which house the most disabled residents spoken of as 'farmyards', places where you need to 'take your bucket and shovel'. It is not so far from that to the books for children which still underline the notion that some of their contemporaries are more like animals than human beings.

In David Rook's *Run Wild, Run Free*, it is only through his relationship with a wild pony that the young hero finally breaks through his severe autistic withdrawal to relate to people. In Eveline Hasler's *Martin is Our Friend*, a small boy who, as we learn on the first two pages, is unable to run, skip, jump, play leapfrog or cops and robbers, or even football in the goal, is only on the way to acceptance by the other children on his block when he manages to soothe a runaway horse. In Roy Brown's *Find Debbie,* the girl in question doesn't manage to break through at all. Instead, in this bleak and damaging tale which manages to condemn the policies of 'community care', suggest that people with mental illnesses are murderers and convey that children with mental handicaps bring nothing but sorrow and despair to all those around them, the Debbie in question is variously described as 'something malignant', 'a changeling', 'a witch in falsely human form', and 'just an animal, something to be put down'. One young woman, whose mental handicap has taken her to a variety of institutions, knows how perception can become practice: 'You can go into a hostel and be hospitalized if you're in a hostel. No freedom, like a little animal or dog. If they say you've got to go to bed, you got to go; you can't go on your own, you're not independent or anything. You come in and they take it all away.'

If people with disabilities have been seen as animals, perception can take them further from human-kind than that. Those whose limitations are particularly severe are commonly called 'vegetables'. Maureen Oswin, in her 1978 study *Children Living in Long Stay Hospitals*, gives one instance of the perception, and with it a snapshot of the practices that grow from it:

> In the spastics' ward, six-year-old Shirley played with her tears, whirling her fingers disconsolately round in them as they puddled on the bare table in front of her. Her actions epitomized a bleak existence. One of the visitors said, 'These children are cabbages' and the others agreed with him, but perhaps it had not occurred to them to look at Shirley and consider that cabbages don't cry.

The people who live with this sort of terminology will take it on board. They will introduce themselves as 'high-grades', to distinguish themselves from the 'low-grades' who live in the back wards — both terms that you might think have more to do with potatoes or tomatoes than they do with human beings. Nor do people whose disabilities are physical escape either perception or practice. It is perhaps no accident that two differing approaches to the running of the residential establishments in which they may find themselves are characterized by Millar and Gwynne, in their influential *A Life Apart*, as 'warehousing' and 'horticultural'.

It is in the responses to the claims of people with severe disabilities to the full range of sexual and emotional relationships that perceptions of them as less than fully human find

83

their touchstone. It is in these relationships, after all, that we find our common humanity, across whatever barriers race, beliefs or national frontiers throw up. It is also in these relationships, just because they are so fundamental, that we are challenged by the notion that people who are clearly further from mental or physical 'perfection' than we ourselves may actually reach a fulfilment which seems greater than our own. What is the response to that claim to be fully human, to that challenge?

In 'The Invalid Mind', Judith Thunem, who has had severe rheumatoid arthritis since she was in her late teens, has this to say:

In his encounter with society, the invalid rarely meets active dislike or disgust. But if he ventures into the world of love, such feelings are not so far off. It happens, on occasion, that a disabled person falls in love with a normal member of society. Sometimes it even happens that this love is reciprocated. It is interesting to observe the different reactions to such — one is tempted to say — a social outrage. One gets the impression that the invalid has more or less committed an indecent act. He isn't supposed to have such feelings. And the 'normal' partner in such a crazy adventure — well, he is hardly considered normal at all. He ought to have his head examined. Some people seem to feel offended at the thought that a 'disabled' person feels the same way as a 'normal' person does. This reaction is not apparent when invalids marry one another. As long as they keep to themselves society doesn't really mind. The invalid may marry another of his kind, and live happily or unhappily ever after. Society doesn't greatly care whether he is happy or unhappy as long as society isn't troubled. A wall is raised between the 'normal' world and the world of the disabled — a wall invisible and hard and cold as unbreakable glass.

The 1970s have brought their own sexual revolution. 'Sex and disability' has become something of a boom industry. Where once there was silence and shuffling, there are conferences, reports and advice centres. Where once there was denial that people with disabilities – 'eternal children' that they were – had sexual lives to lead at all, where once there was the echo of the eugenic era in the belief that even if they did, these should be stamped on for the sake of the human stock, there is a growing awareness that they too are human. It is a stage in the liberation of us all, in the breaking of that glass wall, in overcoming the still formidable barriers that stand between many people with disabilities and their own emotional fulfilment. It is perhaps just worth wondering, in passing, whether any other group of people would put up with such a public, publicized, enquiring going-over of their private lives – whether, for instance, miners would relish public discussion about the effects of shift working and pit-dust on their sexual relationships. In some curious way, the avowals of the new liberalism, in their insistence on technique in isolation from social context, somehow confirm that people with disabilities are not far from 'animals' after all. As one man said: 'The aids and the advice are fine and good. But I can't even get to the places where I might meet someone – and even if I could I wouldn't have enough money to buy them a drink.'

The old perceptions cast their shadow still. Marriage between people with disabilities – far less between them and 'normals' – is still not the end that is devoutly urged on the majority of young people. For the minority, convention can be somehow reversed: sex, most certainly; marriage – is it wise? Marriage brings the possibility of children and people who are mentally retarded have not escaped the eugenic tradition. Mythology insists that they 'breed irresponsibly'; evidence says that they can learn to use contraception responsibly. Mythology says their disability is hereditary; evidence says that this is by no means always so, and that environmental handicap depends to a large extent on the help families receive. Mythology usually wins. And the imagined irresponsibility of young women with severe mental retardation can be countered by a real one among those who have some say in their lives. It is not uncommon for those who live in residential centres to have contraceptive pills administered as part of the day's medicine round, without their knowledge or any explanation of the possible hazards.

More drastic interventions are not only tolerated but may

be accepted as usual. This is what a nine-year-old American girl reported that her mother had told her: 'The girl scout dance isn't safe, because I could have a baby who would be sick like me. But when I'm fifteen I can have an operation and then I can dance.'[2] Despite the assertions of the civil rights lobby, despite the court actions, over twenty American States still had laws permitting involuntary sterilization during the 1970s. If Britain never took that legislative route, it was rejected more because of the impracticability of stamping out all mental defect, than on an assertion of rights. As late as 1975, the English Department of Health, following a much-publicized case in which a judge prohibited the sterilization of a young girl, issued a discussion document on when this operation might be considered proper on a girl (no mention of boys) who was too young to withhold consent to it. The paper raised the question not just for girls under sixteen with mental handicaps, but for those with physical disabilities as well, whether these were hereditary or of the sort, like chronic kidney failure or heart disease, where abortion or child-bearing might damage life or health. The paper raised controversy and indignation; it was quietly dropped. But the question of what really constitutes 'voluntary' sterilization among women whose mental retardation is severe remains to remind us that in some respects at least, some people with disabilities are not yet recognized as fully human.

At its limit, this perception can lead to ultimately final practices. Hitler's extermination of the 'racially valueless' still arouses horror. The agreement between doctor and parents to allow the death of a severely disabled child is deemed a matter of private conscience rather than public debate; it is only occasionally that an individual case will hit the headlines and raise an issue that we prefer to forget. It is not often, in Britain at least, that that issue will come before even a professional audience. Here is one example of the arguments and the practice, from a paediatrician writing in the British medical journal *Lancet* at the end of 1979:

I can remember what a relief it was to be able to tell spina bifida parents of the surgical advances that were going to

86

make life so much better for their new-born, partly paralysed baby, and the faith and hope with which the parents and I watched the stages of repair, valve, tendon transplant, urinary diversion. It was so much easier than having to face the fact that all I could offer, as I do today, is some help in hastening the end of a life which I now have to advise the parent would otherwise be one which is *not a life in any full sense.* The courage of my paraplegic, wheelchair-bound adolescent spina bifidas, with their pressure sores, over-weight, urine bag and chronic renal failure, is sometimes almost unbearable. [my italics]

So he now offers these severely disabled babies careful and loving nursing, and water to satisfy their thirst, together with increasing doses of sedatives, if this is what their parents choose. It is a mark of our unwillingness to debate this issue that the editor of the journal decided to publish the article anonymously.

The practice is as old as human society; it is the perception that goes with it that may change. This doctor, through his own anguish and that of parents, has arrived at his own perception of what constitutes 'life in a full sense'; we are not told what the adolescents with spina bifida have to say. Other doctors have come to their own definitions. So an American team, working in a special care nursery, referred to the concept of 'humanhood', including the capacity to love and be loved, in its own definition, with parents, of children who would not reach that state. A recent working party of the Anglican Church in Canada pursued the definition. It saw human life as consisting in 'the capability of man to relate to himself, to his neighbour and with God'. It defined three categories of life as 'not human': that of the person who is terminally ill, who has lost critical capability, and of the 'newborn infant with gross neurological defects and without even the potential for developing the criteria of human life'. So, it argued:

We are obligated to treat all sentient beings in a humane way, not causing them pain, and, if they are in pain, endeavouring to relieve it. This obligation to treat animals humanely does not mean to most of us that we should treat them as if they were human. Our senses and emotions lead us into the grave mistake of treating human-looking shapes as if they were human, although they lack the least vestige of human behaviour and intellect. In fact the only way to treat [them] humanely is not to treat them as human.

Thus euthanasia would be no crime against its three groups. Everyone of us will have our own reaction to that and there is nothing to say that what we would wish for others we would, finally, wish for ourselves. A woman who has had difficulty walking all her life, for instance, believes strongly that children disabled from birth should be 'let die'. She says bluntly that she would not have wished to be born, that life for her has been endless frustration. But, she adds, she would surely have got somewhere if she had been properly educated; she would love to have worked with others with disabilities, to have married and borne children.

While individuals make their own decisions and act as they can, the collections of individuals which make up societies prefer to talk of preventing disability from arising at all. The aim can't be challenged; the tools are often there; the only possible question can be why they are not better used. If poverty were alleviated and doctors provided better ante-natal and obstetric care, it's been estimated – on the basis of Swedish experience – that the incidence of cerebral palsy in Britain could be reduced by forty per cent. If the English Department of Health had launched a determined campaign at the end of the 1970s to ensure that women had been vaccinated against German measles, the worst epidemic of the disease in years would not have left up to a thousand babies with often grievous mental and physical disabilities in its wake. If industry were safer, it would bring fewer accidents and diseases. The question is one for individuals as well as societies. We all know enough about the disabling 'diseases of affluence'; we all know the possible consequences of mixing driving and drink.

So prevention becomes an important aim, and the perception is pursued in more or less energetic practice. And yet, for some people, the practice brings rather different perceptions. Not so long ago, there was a major national meeting of workers in the field of mental retardation in Canada. It was unusual, in that the organizers had decided, for the first time, to run alongside the main congress another, smaller one for people who were most affected by parental and professional decisions. The programme went well; it was felt to be a step forwards recognition of the rights of people who are mentally retarded. On the last day, there was a splendid and elaborate luncheon. The food was excellent; spirits were high. And if it was unfortunate that there was no room for delegates to the subsidiary conference in the main dining hall, they most certainly were served the same food and had the chance to watch the main proceedings on closed circuit TV. Speeches were made; the congratulations flowed like the wine. As a finale, a cheque was presented to the organizing association by local well-wishers. It was a very large cheque, but then, as the presenter said, on behalf of all those voluntary groups which had raised the money, it was to be used in a very important cause — research into the more effective prevention of mental retardation, 'Canada's number one problem, the greatest scrouge our country faces'.

One young man who heard this on the closed circuit TV went home in a thoughtful frame of mind; he made little answer when his friends asked how he had enjoyed himself. As the days went on, he was evidently upset; the reason was unclear. Finally, his friends felt that his behaviour meant that something was really wrong; this time, they were more successful in finding out what troubled him. He started to talk about the conference, about all that had happened there, the parties, discussions and entertainments. And then he burst out — and this a month after the event — 'They want to get rid of us!'

'For the able-bodied, normal world,' says Paul Hunt:

we are representatives of many of the things that they most fear — tragedy, loss, dark and the unknown. Involuntarily we walk, or more often sit, in the valley of the shadow of death. Contact with us throws up in people's faces the fact of sickness and death in the world, which in themselves are an affront to all our aspirations and hopes. A deformed and paralysed body attacks everyone's sense of well-being and invincibility. People do not want to acknowledge what disability affirms — that life is tragic and we shall all soon be dead. So they are inclined to avoid those who are sick or old, shying from the disturbing reminders of unwelcome reality.

As long ago as the eighteenth century, British children were confirming his point as they learned their alphabet: 'I is an ill man and hated by all.' They still chant their self-protective charms as the ambulance goes by; unlike some others passed on by adults, these do not seem silly to them at all. They still read Frances Hodgson Burnett's *The Secret Garden*, first published in 1911, in which the Victorian perception of disability as suffering bravely borne gives way to a new one: that of disability as bringing death to relationships and to nature itself, its 'cure' coming from nature's own rebirth.

The perception of people with disabilities as 'sick', paradoxically enough, also brings more comfort than any others. It enables our societies to 'get rid of' all the unease that people with disabilities carry for them. It offers an avoidance which is ideal, because it is not only 'humane' but a symbol of caring. It is a solution to the problems posed by 'eternal children' in adult form — for what is the normal way to treat the sick but to offer them a respite from real life? There is even a perfectly respectable range of institutions in which that respite can be lived out — and in which, incidentally, a 'menace' can be contained. And in those who staff them, there are people whose job it is to take the responsibility on themselves. Just what the 'medical' solution has meant to the people who have lived most closely with it is explored in the next two chapters.

7

Institutions and their Inhabitants

> Being in the institution was bad. I got tied up and locked
> up. I didn't have any clothes of my own and no privacy.
> We got beat at times, but that wasn't the worst. The real
> pain came from always being part of a group. I was never
> a person. I was part of a group to eat, sleep and everything.
> As a kid, I couldn't figure out who I was. I was part of a
> group. It was sad.[1]

That young American got his chance to find out who he was,
to establish his personality and stamp it on how he chose to
spend his time. Many thousands of other people who are also
mentally retarded, in his country and all over the Western
world, are living still with the constraints that institutional
living brings. Thousands of people with severe physical disabilities will find in his remembered experience echoes of their
own, as they too find themselves in different institutional
settings they must call 'home'. The institutions may be called
mental handicap hospitals, or State residential centres, or
community residences, or hostels if they house people who
are mentally retarded; they may be called hospitals or 'younger
chronic sick units' or residental homes if they house people
whose disabilities are physical. They may be huge and old and
distant from any ordinary community; they may be home for
twenty or so people and on its fringes. People may have chosen
to live there because they offer a chance to establish a life
independent of their parents; more often, they will be there
because it was the only option open to them. They may feel

they had very little choice in the matter at all, like the young woman who is mentally retarded who said: 'My mother put me away because I couldn't read and write. Then she told me I'm leaving hospital, but I didn't know nothing about it. They said to me "You're being transferred" and I didn't know nothing about it.'

The way of life in these different institutional settings may be more or less fulfilling. For some, they offer a real home and the chance to explore and enjoy their communities. For others, like a man severely disabled as the result of polio and now living with his family, the prospect of ending up in a residential home is, quite simply, 'appalling'; he is determined that he will die rather than go to one. What is sure is that they will seldom offer what people who do not live in them would recognize as an 'ordinary life'. And while those people may find echoes of its particularities in their own remembered experiences − whether of boarding school, life in the armed forces or at college − they will know too that those experiences were of limited duration and mitigated by their continuing contacts with a 'home' outside them. For people who live in institutions, those institutions *are* home, and their contacts outside them may be severely limited by the barriers that the outside environment throws up. How does institutional living measure up to our common notions of what a home should be?

For a start, the living space will most often be geared to groups rather than to individuals; there will be little room for ordinary privacy. Conditions in the large old mental retardation institutions have raised clouds of scandal throughout the 1970s, and a tremendous amount of money and personal energy from staff, in Britain at least, has gone into improving them. But the result is still a ward with bedspaces for thirty people or more and a large 'dayroom'. The appallingly inadequate old lavatories and bathrooms may have been replaced; instead, there may be rows of lavatories with partitions between them, low enough for anyone coming into the room to see exactly who is there and what they are up to, and a number of baths with no more privacy, in place of the one there was before.

For the people who must live with them, such modest improvements are important. 'They don't call it a hospital,

92

they call it our home,' says one man; he talks appreciatively of his new wooden bed, his locker and the personal clothing to put in it, the fact that he even has a bedside lamp and the walls have been newly painted white. But he remembers, too, that when he was young, at home, he had his own room with a wallpaper with flowers on, and he wishes that one day he could have that sort of space again. The lack of privacy can seem total. 'You say something on one of the villas and it's all over the hospital before you can say Jack Robinson,' says one woman with feeling. If she is miserable, she puts her head under the bedclothes and tries not to cry before the others in her room are asleep. Another man agrees with her: it's best not to let the others know if you are unhappy. He counts himself lucky that he has the run of the hospital grounds and can go for a walk, alone, until he feels better.

People living in community homes echo the strains that lack of privacy may bring, and the tensions of living with a group of people you haven't chosen to be with. 'People keep doing the same things, then it starts irritating you and you have to have it out with someone.' Sharing a bedroom can bring its own problems: 'I'd like my own room a bit private and away from all the others, so you don't have to sit together.' In 1979, a group of young Scandinavians who are mentally retarded found this elementary condition of privacy important enough to take to the streets and demonstrate for single rooms.

If residental homes for people who are mentally retarded do not always offer that choice, neither do those for people with severe physical disabilities. Paul Hunt, who had his share of institutional living, outlined what a single room can mean and so what the lack of it denies. It means privacy for entertaining friends and relatives; it means being able to express your personality by having your things around you and deciding on fittings and colour schemes; it means being able to listen to the wireless, to have the window open or shut and the heating on or off; it means being able to go to bed early or late — and it means all this without the nervous strain of constantly adjusting to someone else's conflicting tastes, habits and wishes. When they have their own room, people have far more privacy, both physically and in personal affairs — things that are highly valued in our society but sadly lacking in the average institution, especially where residents are dependent on staff for intimate daily needs. Perhaps the most important gain of all is having a piece of personal territory to which boundaries can be drawn. There seems to be a fundamental animal and human need to possess an area which is in effect an extension of oneself. Without it, the adult human tends to be too insecure to form a constructive and stable network of personal relationships.[2]

So for some people, institutional living may offer little encouragement to friendship. The woman who remembers only one friend from twenty-five years of life in a mental retardation institution would not be alone in that; she talks instead of 'a crowd like that, who don't understand your problems.' A middle-aged man who lives in a community residence has not yet, either, found the relationships to replace the one that was the most important to him:

> Your mother's your best friend. When you've lost her, you've lost a good friend. There's nothing like being at home. My mother was good to me and I was good to her. My mother was used to arguing with me, but I never took no notice. I used to go into the other room and have a laydown. When I lost my mother, why I got sisters and they don't come up to see me and I go down to see them . . . When they get married, they've got no time for you. I don't eat so much when I go home, I lost my conscience, I can't help it. Your mother's your mother. When you ain't got your mother, you're done for.

People who live in institutions may get the chance to join a group outing; they may get the chance to be entertained by groups of volunteers who bring their guitars and their goodwill. But when group meets group, it is not individual friendships that usually come out of it.

There may be little encouragement, either, for people to form relationships which are closer than this, if they so choose.

Even when people do have their own room, their privacy may be constrained by the staff's habit of knocking and then simply walking in without waiting for an invitation. For the sake of 'safety', it is rare for rooms to have locks on the doors. Young people with physical disabilities will talk of staff who 'treat you like children, never take you seriously', and not only burst into your room but switch on the lights in a darkened television room. What is known drearily as 'unofficial cohabitation' may be tolerated, but the 'official' variety — for those among whom this would be a 'normal' choice — is rare. There are practical constraints: some people will be able to move into a double room if they marry; others may find themselves constantly engaged. In mental retardation institutions, there may be less ambiguity. 'Sex?' said one man; 'Oh yes, there is some, but it's not serious because it's not reported on the ward.' Others have found their own way round the conventions that say that men and women can meet only in the formal atmosphere of chaperoned dances and work. 'Us never got caught once,' remembers one woman who has since married the man she met in such an institution. 'We used to get out night times in the wood, and then if we heard someone coming, I'd run one way and he'd go over the hedge.'[3]

In the end, the most important relationships for people who live in residential institutions may be with those who staff them. And while those relationships may be based on co-operation, respect and friendship, they may also be based on a hierarchy which divides the institutional world clearly into 'helpers' and 'helped'.

People who have lived in British mental retardation institutions for many years will tell you that life in them has changed a great deal over the past decade or so. 'I've been able to go anywhere I like for six years now. When I first went, you couldn't pick up a pin — it was horrible,' remembers one woman. The old rules were inflexible. 'We used to go out three on a pass,' says one man:

> You weren't allowed to leave your partners, oh no, you weren't allowed to leave your partners. You got to be back at six o'clock; if you're not back at six o'clock, if you leave

it a bit too late, your lost your half day for good, sometimes for good altogether. You weren't allowed to leave the town, weren't allowed to go out of the district, only when you were with your parents.

Life for him has become relatively simple since the old Mental Deficiency Act was replaced by the 1959 Mental Health Act and overnight, he and all the thousands of others, became 'voluntary' instead of 'detained' inhabitants of their hospitals. Now all that matters is knowing how to work the system. 'All the staff like me because I help them a lot. Then they help me a lot. I ask for an all day pass and they say "yes" and I go.'

Some people speak highly of the staff, particularly those who have spent many years with them: 'The nurses haven't let me down. They've given me great pressure to go my own way, live as I want to, keep myself. If people like to put themselves forward, no one knows what can be done until they speak their mind. Nurses help people who want to be helped.' But speaking your mind can be difficult; often it is more a question of obeying the staff than discussing things with them. That can be complicated when they have different notions of how things should be done. One woman remembers two nurses, each in charge of the ward for half a week and one with far more traditional ideas than the other: 'We used to call it obeying the Ancient and Modern. They say that too many cooks spoil the broth, and quite right too.' But as the man who worked on the staff for his all day pass knew, you mustn't give them cheek: 'I call them sir sometimes, for a joke, and saulte. But you have to be careful. It's like the army, you see, the staff are in charge – that's why they wear uniforms.'

Staff have a whole range of sanctions to bolster their authority, and people can feel powerless against them. One woman remembers how one Sunday she and a group of friends decided they wouldn't get up to help on the ward at the usual time of 6.30, but would have a lie-in until it was time to get ready for church. 'We wouldn't make any beds, we were in trouble. If the staff ask, you've got to give answer to it. If you don't do as you are told, you know what'll happen – you'll get your punishment.' For her that usually meant going

96

early to bed — and, at the age of thirty-four, she went, because she knew she had to. There is very little appeal against the authority of the people in immediate charge, so if they decide to stop your money for infringement of rules or unsuitable behaviour, that's what they do. Sanctions can be more severe than that, as one young woman found out after a spell in a padded room that seemed more like punishment than 'therapy' to her: 'It's horrible, there's nothing to do but sleep, sleep, sleep. It's very cold, you couldn't go to the toilet, there's a pot in there. You get a pot and a mattress, no blankets, no window, food pushed through the door. Nobody came to talk to me, not even the doctor. "Here's your food, eat it!" but they won't talk to you.' The days become filled with a routine that has little of choice about it. One woman remembers her twenty-five years in hospital like this: 'Up at 5.30, dress the cripples — I was a slave to them — occupational therapy, making rugs and tea cosies, nine to twelve, tea at six, bed by ten. It was terrible really, but you get used to it in time. You wouldn't dare say no. The sister was shocking. If you had the ward door open, you could hear her shout down the corridor.'

If people are left with a feeling of powerlessness in their everyday lives, they may feel powerless too about their future. 'If you're in the ward for very long, staff and everything,' says one young woman, 'you're not allowed to think for yourself. No independence, privacy or self-respect. You're told to do this and do that, you're always in a row, go and wash the floors and scrub the kitchen. It's very strict, you feel like running away from places like that. You can't stand it after a time . . .' But she also knew she had nowhere to run to. Many people who live in institutions wish they could live somewhere else, like the man who said this:

My business is to get away, right away altogether so I can forget all about my lifetime in the past. You can't help thinking about it because you're still in the same hospital where you was. You must get right away, so you could forget. I'm looking forward to the future, that's what my ambition is, to get things organized if I can.

He could and he did. But others may not find it so easy.

I know I keep the boundaries – I don't smoke, I don't drink, I'm allowed to go out at night. I go to church on my own. But I have to come back, don't I, worse luck? There's no alternative. Where are you going to go?

The question could be echoed by many people in the different sorts of institution which cater for those with severe physical disabilities. The conditions of their lives may not be as extreme as those of people in the large mental retardation institutions; the deadening routines of those places may be replaced by a sapping sameness in the restrictions of everyday life. But they too may be assured that this is their home, and find that visitors have to be out by a certain hour, or that there are subtle sanctions against coming in late, or that the time they get up in the morning is constrained by the shifts of the staff who are there to help them, or that there is little choice in either the timing or content of meals. Paul Hunt again:

In the hospitals and homes I have lived in, one rarely sees any physical cruelty. But I have experienced enough of other kinds of subtly corrupting behaviour. There are administrators and matrons who have had people removed on slight pretexts, who try to break up ordinary friendships if they don't approve of them. There are the staff who bully those who cannot complain; who dictate what sort of clothes people should wear, who switch the TV off in the middle of the programme and will take away 'privileges' – like getting up for the day – when they choose.

He was angered enough by the countless times he had seen people hurt, treated as less than people, told what to do and how to behave by those 'whose only claim to do this came from prejudice and their power over them'.

There is nothing 'normal' about a place which is home for its inhabitants but which dictates even when and what they eat or what they wear, which is run by routines which they have not chosen and which they cannot change, which offers little encouragement to ordinary relationships of cooperation and trust, but is based instead on hierarchy and rule. But there is nothing 'normal' either in the perceptions that are behind these places and breathe through their bricks and mortar still.

The large institutions which grew up all over the Western world to house people who are mentally retarded — and are even now being built both there and in countries which are only beginning to develop their own services — may have started with a mixture of motives. As early optimism about education and even 'cure' was disappointed, they became needed not just to protect their inhabitants from the demands of their society, but to protect that society from a menace to its health. As they proliferated, it is the perception of their inhabitants as less than human, as even animal, that has allowed the quite appalling physical environment that they have so often provided. But it has been the perception of their inhabitants as 'sick' which has sustained them as a respectable and even 'humane' provision, which enabled Britain, for instance, to transform them overnight into 'hospitals' and their workers into 'nurses' when the National Health Service was set up after the Second World War. If that particular administrative decision is still in force to colour perceptions in one country, others are still living with the inheritance in the bricks and mortar of their own institutional provision. And if the community residences of different sorts that have sprung up over the past decade or so have taken a revulsion from that older institutional model as their starting-point, they have also often built in an echo of the old perception. Their inhabitants may not be defined as 'sick'. But they may often be seen as 'helpless', out of the running of 'normal' expectations, in need of a dictated regime rather than cooperative guidance: why else, after all, are they there, if not for the fact that they can't cope with life's demands?

The perception of people with severe physical disabilities as 'sick' has been more pervasive yet, the practices that result from it even more clear-cut. The 'younger chronic sick', after all, is what these people have been officially known as in Britain over the years — there is even the 1970 Chronically Sick and Disabled Persons Act on the statute book to drum the point home. So it could seem inevitable, and even right, that the only alternative for people who could no longer live in their own homes should become the 'chronic ward' of a hospital – a place where doctors and nurses oversaw the lives of a random mixture of frail, elderly people and younger ones who also had nowhere else to live. It could seem nothing but humane that when there was an outcry about the need for alternative accommodation for the younger people at the end of the 1960s – the older ones being still assumed to 'fit' into this way of life – the solution was to provide special 'younger chronic sick' hospital units rather than anything else. The provision has been condemned as 'a prison' by those who might one day have to live with it. But it grew, and by the end of the 1970s it was home for some fifteen hundred people.

More than ten times that number live in residential homes which have nothing to do with hospital at all. Yet they too carry their echo of the perception of sickness. They may even, in dubbing the person in charge as 'matron', make this explicit. And they too may take as their starting-point the 'helplessness' of the inhabitants, their inability to perform certain basic physical tasks perceived as an inability to share any 'normal' expectations: why else, after all, should they be there? For some observers at least, the perception is harsher yet. In *A Life Apart*, their influential study of different residential institutions for people with severe physical disabilities, Millar and Gwynne take as their major thesis that the uncomfortable job of these places is to 'cater for the socially dead during the interval between social death and physical death'. Their inhabitants, so they argue, have no role in their wider society, no positive social status, and that is tantamount to social death: 'To be admitted to one of these institutions is to enter a kind of limbo in which one has been written off as a member of society but is not yet physically dead.'

The perceptions are powerful. They are also false. Conditions that bring disability may bring the need for medical treatment in the initial stages; disability may indeed be the result of disease. But that is not at all to say that people with disabilities are 'ill' any more than the rest of the population; the vast majority are living in their own homes, getting on with

100

their lives without benefit of either medical supervision or constant nursing care. People who have severe disabilities may be unable to do certain things. But being unable to take yourself to the lavatory doesn't in any way mean you are unable to choose the pattern of your life within the inevitable confines of disability: being limited in your understanding doesn't mean that you are not either encouraged or hurt in your sense of yourself, or that you are incapable of learning choice. Millar and Gwynne may see people who live in residential institutions as 'socially dead'; they know that they are trying to live their lives.

For the world outside the institutions, the perceptions serve their purpose: they justify and sustain the exclusion of people who are disquieting with a humane inevitability. For the people who staff the institutions, the perceptions may be a path out of their own dilemma, charged as they are to keep their charges tidily, economically and kindly out of the way; they may find their own defences in the institutional routines they throw up to keep a distance between themselves and sickness, helplessness and death. Doctors and nurses, whose entire training and expectation is geared to hope of 'cure', may find that the only way to manage this 'incurable' population, this remainder of the limits of their skills, is to do precisely that — to manage the physical needs of their charges and in doing so avoid the challenge to their perceptions that individual strengths, weaknesses and needs throw up. For the people on the receiving end of this care, the perceptions can bring layer upon layer of handicap to overlay their disabilities; perceived and treated as 'helpless', helpless is what, in larger or smaller ways, they will tend to become. And then the world outside the institutions will be able to confirm its original perceptions. The cycle of expectation will be complete.

Just how it works is most dramatically illustrated by the story of what happens to the four thousand or so children who live in British mental retardation hospitals. Some of them are there because they can no longer stay with their families and no alternative home is on offer. But others, according to the official view, are there because they need the help that 'only a hospital can provide'.

Yet in her 1978 study of children living in the 'special care' wards of eight of these hospitals, Maureen Oswin found that 'special care' was precisely what they did not get. They lacked even the most basic medical attention; in five hospitals, children were suffering from 'what can only be described as the poverty conditions of the nineteenth century' — chronic catarrh, runny ears, sore eyes, skin diseases, bad teeth, stomach upsets and worms. Even elementary aids were lacking: in five hospitals, again, there were not enough wheelchairs for the children and those there were, were old and broken. Very few children had been assessed for sensory handicaps, let alone provided with the aids that could help alleviate these. The corrective surgery rhat could have helped them had often simply not been done; physical deformities were grossly exacerbated too by lack of physiotherapy. There was no speech therapy, although it could have helped many children eat more easily. There was precious little occupational therapy, although others could perhaps have learned to feed, wash and dress themselves, and others again to grasp. In only one hospital did the children get any attention from a psychologist; only ninety of the hundred and fifty-three of compulsory school age were getting full-time education. And although the children got, on average, one hour of physical attention in every ten, they got only five minutes of 'mothering'.

Some of this neglect had to do with severe and continuing shortages of staff. But some of it, too, had to do with the way the children were perceived. Doctors concentrated their energy on the more 'hopeful' outpatient clinics; corrective surgery was often seen as 'not worth it'. Physiotherapists chose to spend their time with others who were more responsive. Speech therapists felt they should give their energy to, say, businessmen recovering from a stroke. The psychologist in one hospital said his time should go to people who could earn a place outside it. The social workers who might have been expected to show concern for the appalling standards of child-care on the wards commonly saw this as none of their concern; one had nothing to do with them because 'these children will never be discharged'.

The result was entirely predictable: the children, already

very seriously disabled, were also grossly handicapped by this almost complete lack of help. Their small abilities and potentials were not encouraged – so they became harder to look after. The hard-pressed nurses made no demands on them because they could see little future for them. Teaching them to play and encouraging the development of relationships through this became 'a waste of time'. Maintaining ward routines took precedence over the children's needs: 'If they weren't here, it would be OK, but we can't do our work when they're around,' said one nurse when the administration of the ward was interrupted by an unexpected school holiday. The nurses defined their job in terms of bare maintenance: 'there's nothing we can do for them except keep them clean, warm and fed.' The most common expectations of the children were that they should keep still in their chairs, keep fairly quiet, eat quickly and not spit their food out, not smell too badly and sleep well at night. The goal of treatment was often simply that they should fit well into the adult wards across the campus when they grew up. And here the staff are likely to 'succeed', for the children will have no alternative at all. And the world will see in this 'inevitable' progress a confirmation of the need of 'special care wards' for another generation of children with profound disabilities. It will forget that children who are offered individual relationship and the professional help they need will begin to grow within the limitations that their disabilities must impose; it will forget that it is not only possible but 'normal' to offer them, as any child, the possibility of that growth.

The situation of these children in hospital is extreme; when they grow up, they will be among the most severely disabled people in the country. But their situation illustrates too, with a clarity and starkness made possible by their extreme vulnerability to other people's perceptions of them, the damage that the cycle of expectation can inflict. The difference between them and others who find themselves in institutional settings may be only one of degree.

So people who live on the 'backwards' of mental retardation institutions, offered conditions and relationships more suited to animals than to human beings, will begin to behave in ways which are indeed bizarre and can simply reinforce the original perception. By no means all such institutions have yet learned the lesson taught with such clarity by the Scandinavians in the 1960s, when they started providing environments fit for human habitation and found that their inhabitants started living up to the expectations inherent in them. So people treated as incapable of deciding what to wear or eat will have little sense of themselves and their potential for operating in their environment. So people who lived with the perversions of ordinary expectations that can colour institutional life will be cut off from chances to understand the ordinary world. There is the story of the man who was sent back to hospital from a community home because his behaviour was intolerable 'outside'. It turned out that no one had thought to teach him that the open masturbation which was 'normal' on the hospital ward was not acceptable elsewhere; now he masturbates in private like everyone else and has put the hospital behind him for ever.

The examples may seem extreme; but they are characteristic enough of the everyday experience of thousands of people. And they can find their echoes in other residential settings, too, as a woman with severe physical disabilities has found out on her move from a home where everything was done — and kindly — for its inhabitants, to one where they are expected to take responsibility for their own everyday lives. She fought for the move, she revels in the freedom to come and go as she pleases, in the determination of the staff to act as encouragers of individuality and not guardians of a common pattern. But she also knows what it is like, and this in her mid-thirties, to have to reckon for the first time with the price of a pound of cheese. She knows too that she is now living up to the expectations around her, just as she lived down to them before.

And if this is true on one level, it is true on others. In a home where the warden treats sexuality as a sort of infectious disease — 'once one starts, they're all at it' — talks disparagingly of 'snogging' and 'necking', frisks the young men's belongings for contraceptives and concludes 'we're not hard on them, they've got the woods to go to', it's not perhaps surprising that the emotional lives of the inhabitants have the characteristics that enable observers to confirm their impression of them as immature and 'unable' to form lasting relationships. In a home where the staff feel free to fling open people's bedroom doors at will, or take casual visitors tramping through the house, it is not surprising if the inhabitants end up with little sense of pride in their person or their environment.

At the limit, people may conclude that they can influence what goes on in their own home very little indeed. A recent exchange of correspondence in the *Cheshire Smile*, the journal of the Cheshire Homes, Britain's largest chain of establishments for people with physical disabilities, illustrates the point. A suggestion that the current system of homes run by wardens and matrons should be replaced by one in which residents themselves took responsibility brought a flurry of replies. Most of them were adamant that the present system worked; fewer suggested that residents should take more joint responsibility; some pointed out that the possibility was there, but that residents did not choose to take it. One woman, writing on behalf of her husband and herself, was clear:

> We dare not start to think what our lives would be like without a Matron, or someone in charge. Just think. Some fellow residents can't move, let alone help run their Home. We agree every handicapped person needs to have a certain amount of independence, but the Home would be in an uproar without a Matron, or someone in charge, and this would take away the friendly and homely feeling which I am sure we could not do without.

Others know that not being able to move unaided need be no bar to taking their share of responsibility, that disability need be no bar to creating a home.

Others again know that keeping that reality alive in an institutional setting may be anything but easy. 'Unless he fights a constant battle to retain his intellectual integrity and sense of purpose,' says Louis Battye in 'The Chatterley Syndrome',

> as the years go by [the congenital cripple] will gradually feel the atmosphere of the [home] closing in on him, as it did in the chronic ward, shrinking his horizons to the limits

of the house and grounds, a condition in which trivial details of the home's day-to-day routine assume a disproportionate importance. In spite of the efforts to arouse or retain his interest in life, he will feel boredom and apathy creeping over him like a slow paralysis, eroding his will, dulling his criticial wits, dousing his spirit, killing his independence. The temptation to sit day after day, year after year, with the same little clique in the same corner of the room, doing the same things, thinking the same thoughts, making and listening to the same banal remarks, becomes almost irresistible. In a subtler, more civilized way than in the chronic ward, he will have become institutionalized.

The particular dangers of institutional living, the handicap that it can superimpose on disability, have been the subject of acres upon acres of studies and texts; 'institutionalization' is an accepted consequence of living in institutions. 'The larger a community of infirm or defective persons is, the more they act upon each other; the more salient become the pecularities flowing out of their infirmity; the more they become like each other and the more unlike ordinary persons − hence the less fitted for ordinary society.' So said Samuel Gridley Howe in an article on handicapped children almost a hundred years ago. People who are blind and mute, said the Massachusetts Board of State Charities, often exhibit morbid tendencies.

Now these are lessened and their morbid effects corrected in each individual, by intimate intercourse with persons of good and normal condition − that is, by general society; while they are strengthened by associating closely and persistently with others having the like infirmity . . . Guided by this principle, we should, in providing for the instruction and training of these persons, have the association among them as little as possible, and counteract its tendencies by encouraging association and intimacy with common society. They should be kept together no more closely and no longer than is necessary for their special instruction; and there should be no attempts to build up permanent asylums for them, or to favour the establishment of communities composed wholly, or mainly, of persons subject to a common infirmity.

And that, in 1866.

And now, at the end of another century, we are trying to undo the damage that so many institutions have created and create still. The institutional reform that was the first response to the appalling conditions in many, especially the ones which have housed people who are mentally retarded, is increasingly seen as no longer enough, by both 'experts' and inhabitants.

> They asked me if I enjoyed being called a resident, and I told them I'd always been a resident, as far as I'm concerned whatever you say won't make any difference. We'll still be patients here, won't we? It doesn't make any difference, does it? It would be nice to be called a resident if I went somewhere else.

People who are mentally retarded are picking up a new rhetoric, like this young American: 'All people are created equal and have the right to live as well as others in the community and fight for rights.' People with physical disabilities are rejecting the isolation from the ordinary range of opportunities that institutional life can impose.

So by the end of the 1970s, 'deinstitutionalization' was a key word in North American policies; offering people the opportunity to lead 'as normal a life as possible' has become, throughout the West, an axiomatic springboard of provision, whatever their disability. Models of service and support to replace the old institutional patterns, or offer people real choice in their way of living, are making the abolition of the traditional institution, and all that it symbolizes by way of rejection, all it carries by way of damaging perception, a perfectly possible and exciting prospect. We shall be looking at alternatives to institutional inevitability in the next section. But before we get there, there is a hurdle to cross.

The institutions did not spring from nowhere, fully armed. They were created and have been sustained by a cycle of

107

expectation whose roots go deep. And while that cycle can only be dented by alternatives to traditional institutional patterns, it is useless to think that simply to help people move from bad old institution A to good new setting B will be enough to break it. Already we can see that the alternatives to traditional institutions are re-creating, in some places and at some times, some of their worst features — and already some people are seizing on this to 'prove' that traditional solutions are inevitable ones, that the handicaps imposed in the past must be an inevitable concomitant of severe disability in the future. It is not much good congratulating ourselves on offering people who are mentally retarded, for instance, their chance to lead 'as normal a life as possible in their community' if that life must be lived, as it must in a spanking new British hostel, surrounded by a special school, two hospitals, a cemetry, a crematorium and a municipal garbage dump: the old perceptions are still getting their confirmation in practice. It is not much good talking of 'as normal a life as possible' to people with physical disabilities if their community continues to throw up physical barriers to block their access to it.

If the battle against institutional inevitability as the end of the line for people with disabilities is one for us all, it is especially one for the different professional 'helpers' who have mushroomed over the past decades to enable those people to share in common opportunities and choices. For it is professional workers who in large part have the power to sustain or dent the cycle of expectation, not just for people who live in institutions, but for anyone who comes into contact with them. The relationship between people with disabilities and the professional 'carers' is what the next chapter is about.

8

The Cycle of Expectation

An administrator in the hospital service was organizing a series of visits to residential units for people with severe physical disabilities.

> At one home we were taken to see the assessment centre kitchen and left there to await the arrival of the occupational therapist. When she arrived, she completely ignored the others, took no notice at all of my attempts at introductions, but simply fell on me, literally pawing at my clothes as if I were a doll, telling me how lucky I was to be having a day out and what a pretty dress I had on.

Why this extraordinary behaviour? It's a safe bet that it was brought on because the administrator was in a wheelchair. Occupational therapists can be handicapped in their understanding that some people with disabilities aren't simply grist to their professional mill.

A social scientist was also, as it happens, visiting a home for people with severe disabilities. (And yes, the inhabitants of such places do get fed up with strangers tramping around — wouldn't anyone?) This social scientist was making an inquiry into life in places like this. Imagine his surprise when a member of staff, not waiting to hear his explanation of why he was there, started to bundle him off towards the bedroom and assure him that he would soon settle down. Why this extraordinary behaviour? It's not unlikely that it was brought on by the fact that the social scientist happens to be very severely disabled, and can communicate only through a sign board. Staff of residential homes can be handicapped by their assumption that people whose disabilities are as severe as this 'ought' to be candidates for their care. The social scientist, as it happens, had a perfectly good home of his own to go back to.

A telephone-operator-cum-receptionist enjoyed her job well enough. There was just one snag. The doctor in whose office she worked would insist, every time he walked past her desk in the reception hall, on giving her a little pat on the shoulder and saying: 'Ah, Jane, I don't know what we would do without you!' Every morning, it seemed to her, he would say the same thing; every afternoon he would repeat it and every time he introduced her to someone passing through as well. She started to wait for it and she didn't wait in vain. It was driving her crazy. She puzzled over his extraordinary behaviour, and found it made no sense. She assumed that without her, he would simply hire another receptionist. Eventually it occurred to her that if she was having trouble with the doctor, he was also having trouble with her. It struck her that such an evident reminder of the limitations of the medical art as herself — she has severe cerebral palsy — would be bound to make the doctor uncomfortable, not least because a 'failure' like her was doing him a useful service.

None of us is at our best in our relationships with the 'helping professionals'. We meet them in the first place, after all, just because we are not at our best. We are vulnerable to their power and superior expertise. We often make ourselves more vulnerable by taking off our clothes for them. We tell them all sorts of intimate details we would never normally confide to strangers. We do so because on the whole we trust that they will comfort what ails us, deliver the service they promise and let us regain the responsibility for our own lives that we have temporarily relinquished to them. Sometimes we may be disappointed; we may get to mistrust their power and see in it an abuse of our mind, body or wallet; we may see their 'help' as a conspiracy for status; we may try to redress the balance of their power and our helplessness by taking them to court. Either way, we will usually be glad to see the back of both them and the weakness that brought us to them in the first place.

For people with disabilities, these already complicated

relationships may be more complicated yet. They may find that they need them over much longer periods than usual, either because they can do with some of the services that the professional workers promise, or because without them they cannot gain their passport to 'ordinary' opportunities. They may find that their path is studded by 'special' services which have grown up in the wake of the perception of them as perennially 'sick' and so in need of special attention and care. So their relationships with the helping professions may be of far greater importance to them than other people's. If people with disabilities can get such distorted responses from professional workers when they are simply going about their business, what do others meet as they seek help?

For a start, there is nothing to say that the perception of people with disabilities as 'sick' is likely to increase professional understanding of their needs. Indeed, because doctors and nurses too are trained to 'cure', the 'incurable' may be the last thing they can properly tackle. Because they are trained to put right the bits of people which go wrong, rather than see the whole person, they may be particularly likely to assume that an irreparable inability in one area must mean that the whole person is 'helpless'. Even when their contribution to helping people rebuild their lives is invaluable, the concentration on one aspect of rehabilitation may distort the process; even the best of spinal units sometimes has little to offer people who seek sexual and emotional counselling.

So people with disabilities may not meet the understanding from medical services that might be expected from the large part that these services can, one way and another, play in their lives. Many of us would recognize the experience of one woman who is deaf with the hospital service:

One hospital treated me as a normal, responsible adult, which is exactly what I hope for. But the other gave me the most miserable time I've ever had in my life. It was through complete lack of sympathy and understanding on the part of two sisters — so I think a case could be made for telling sisters something about the deaf, though I would have expected them to know . . . I was put between two patients

111

who were unable to communicate, so I was completely marooned. I was never warned of any treatment I was to have, or had anything explained to me. The night sister was actively rude to me when I asked if I could have a sleeping pill; I feel vibration, in fact I'm much more sensitive than a hearing person, so I hardly slept the first night I was in hospital . . . I felt very much at a disadvantage, as I dislike talking to more than one person at once and the consultants, charming and courteous though they were, always brought a 'bodyguard' with them; one of them brought five people and all I wanted to do was dive under the bedclothes . . . Deaf people are very reluctant to complain among hearing people, in case they can't follow everything that is said.

You don't have to be deaf to find insensitivity in hospitals, or lack of communication either.

The lack of medical understanding can have the most devastating effects, particularly as it is so often to doctors that people first turn for help, or to whom they are first turned, and who, in Britain at least, are the people who may hold the passport to all sorts of other specialist and professional services, and even financial help.

So a woman who had a severe stroke in her middle years left hospital with no information at all on how she could rebuild her life. She and her husband between them worked out all sorts of practical aids to daily living. They found out after three years that she was exempt from having to pay for medicines. They have re-established their life. But she still wonders why, when she left hospital, no one put her in touch with help or even gave her a leaflet which indicated how other people have coped. 'We feel it very sad that having suffered the tragedy of a stroke it appears to be no one's job to tell you what you are entitled to and how to go about getting it; you have to find out and fight for yourself.'

One woman who has had a severe and undiagnosed ailment in her knees for the past two-and-a-half years — 'the lack of knowledge is crippling in itself' — has never, she says, been asked by any doctor or specialist she has seen how she *feels*. And she feels very bad. 'I jokingly asked my GP for a psychiatrist and then told him I needed one. As I was crying, it surely cannot have been taken as a joke the second time. Still no counselling was offered until I found some myself. Having asked a medical social worker for help, which proved fruitless, I do not know where else to ask for opportunities and services.' She would not be the only one to find that doctors can be short on understanding: 'Doctors particularly', as another woman says wryly, 'are very bad at understanding that unhappiness may not always be caused by our disability, but by the problem of what to have for supper!'

Understanding is meant to be part of the stock-in-trade of the social worker. They may have plenty of it but little practicality: 'They are all very nice and sympathetic,' says one middle-aged woman with cerebral palsy who lives with her now ageing mother. 'They will come and talk for hours. Then they go back and make long duplicated reports and nothing happens unless we keep on and on making a nuisance of ourselves.' Or they may not seem to understand at all. So a man who contacted his local social services office to seek help with getting his ceiling painted was treated instead to a lengthy visit which had to do with the need the social worker saw for him to come to terms with the fact that he had, some years ago, broken his spine. So a woman who quite badly wanted to discuss the particular strains of living with a disability that fluctuated in the restrictions it imposed was treated instead to a bright homily about the different bath aids now on the market.

It is not just an individual quota of understanding that professional workers bring to their relationship with people who have disabilities. It is also an expectation that they have learned to hold through their own training and experience. And while that expectation can hold a valuable blend of encouragement and realism, it can also be damagingly low. People with disabilities may find themselves faced by professional expectations throughout their lives; they can meet them at any point along them. Either way, they will be, to a greater or lesser degree, caught, simply because at so many critical points they may find themselves relying on professional intervention, whether they particularly choose it or not.

'The paediatrician just says: "The poor old girl won't come on much — see you in six months". The GP said: "Put her in residential care and forget about her". It was horrifying.' And again: 'Doctors treat you like illiterates. The specialist just sits there, reads a report on his desk, looks at him and that's it for six months.' Mothers whose children have severe disabilities have been reporting experiences like this over very many years. But those comments were made at the end of the 1970s. So children can start their lives with very little hope, and their parents with very little understanding of how best to help them. Lack of information is the commonest complaint that parents make, though the situations they are coping with may be extremely difficult. 'It was a real traumatic experience. You never knew what each day would bring. The welfare came once every blue moon or yellow Saturday, but that was no good.'[1]

Sooner or later, children with a severe disability will be officially diagnosed as such and this ascertainment will most usually qualify them for a place in a special school. The expectations of this 'special' service do not seem to be high: it is only comparatively recently that it was reported as an educational service at all in official texts, rather than a 'welfare' service, lumped in with the school meals and milk figures. So one mother whose son of ten has spina bifida is discovering that his special school has a shorter day than a 'normal' one and that there is no provision for its students to take higher public examinations, or indeed any science at all. She is finding that the emphasis of the school is on keeping the children happy rather than worrying about their future prospects. But she does worry about her son's, since his intellect is his only resource; she does worry that the school psychologists tell her that his IQ is falling and will continue to do so as he goes through the system; she does wonder whether they are right when they say it was 'artifically high' when he came to school because he came from an 'advantaged home', or whether in fact it is now 'artificially low'. She does ask: 'Why must my son have to suffer this extra handicap?'[2]

It is a question that researchers have asked too, as they have discovered that teachers in special schools for children with physical disabilities tend to overrate what the children have achieved and make too many allowances for their disabilities, as they have discovered that once the children transfer to ordinary schools, freed from the 'special' cycle of expectation, they make rapid progress. It is a question that young people who have been through the system themselves will ask when they look back on their special schooling, on how 'being happy' was rated higher than working, when they remember the shock of moving from an easy top place in a 'special' class to somewhere near the bottom of an ordinary one. It is a question that young people ponder in other countries and other situations. 'I like most of my teachers except for the mentally retarded one,' says one young man at a junior high school in the United States: 'I hate her class because she ain't a regular teacher. She doesn't really teach — I don't think she expects us to learn nothing. In high school it'll be better because there ain't any retarded teacher there.'[3]

'We are careful in our leavers' preparation,' says the headmaster of a school for children with severe physical disabilities, 'not to promise opportunities and we encourage the pupils to think of lower options.' Very often, they will not have much choice. Special schools, which might be thought most in need of good careers services, are far less likely than others to have any service at all. The preparation for work they offer may be extremely limited and reflect a traditional and stereotyped view of what constitutes 'suitable' employment. So the British National Deaf Children's Society has recently found a heavy reliance on skills like typing and domestic work for girls and wood and metal work for boys in special schools and units for deaf children.

This cycle of expectation may spiral on when young people leave school; they may meet it in the very people whose job it is to help them find employment. They may, like one sixteen-year-old, find themselves on a special training course for school-leavers; they might even, like him, get written up in a magazine designed for professional rehabilitation workers, under a heading like 'Brian amazes the experts'. The reason for their amazement was that this young man had, during the course, built a go-kart powered by a motor-cycle engine — and that with spina bifida! As he had already been stripping down and

115

rebuilding motor cycles for two years, as he rode his own, their amazement was completely ill-placed. The only amazing thing about this story is that a professional journal should, in 1980, be perpetuating the expectations of helplessness that lie behind it.

Others may find help from the 'special' Disablement Resettlement Officers whose job it is, in Britain, to find employment for people with disabilities – or not, as the case may be. One woman remembers going to her DRO for advice when, after three years in her first job, she thought it was time to move on and up. 'What a mistake that was. I was told in no uncertain terms that I should consider myself fortunate to be employed, and cast all thoughts of progress from my mind. I have never approached a DRO in regard to employment since that day, and obtained my next four jobs independently.' Others may be less lucky. A young man with a psychology degree reckons that, despite his uncertain balance, he can think of himself as 'a person first and disabled second'.

But when I go to the Job Centre, I can't be treated like any client. I am straight away sent to see the DRO – who, mark my words, is 'in the know' about what disabled people can do. He is at a loss to place me in any job suitable to a graduate. The trouble with being seen as disabled first is that somehow one internalizes it and begins to see onself in the same way.

So as his search for work goes on, he finds he is becoming less and less confident in his own abilities.

Some people don't even get as far as this, but end up in a 'special' training centre set up for people who are mentally retarded. The first national survey of these places in England and Wales, during the 1970s, found a considerable confusion of expectation among those who ran them. They gave no less than thirty aims for the centres, but none of them was mentioned by even half of them. Less than half cited work training as an aim; forty-three per cent mentioned social education and almost the same proportion 'developing potential to the maximum'. They didn't. Only a third of their workers who graduated to employment in the survey year used the skills they had learned at the centre. The centres hardly shone as educational establishments either: people were more likely to stick with the skills they brought when they arrived than to learn new ones. Nor was individual ability always encouraged: while twenty-seven per cent of workers were able to use public transport, only fourteen per cent actually did. Perhaps the names these workers carried sum up most concisely the way the centres and the opportunities they provide are seen. They are dubbed 'trainees'; more recently, they have sometimes been called 'students'. Either way, they are locked into a state of not-quite-adulthood. A large number of them would rather be somewhere else. As one young American who works under much the same sort of system, says: 'I work in a workshop folding boxes − contract work. I really don't like to say this, but it's boring. It's easy and it's not challenging.'

Some people, whether because of the severity of their disability or because of their family commitments, do not aspire to work at all. They may then qualify for one of the benefits that the State provides. In Britain they may need a doctor's assessment for this. And they may find, in seeking it, that the cycle of expectation is complete. So married women who apply for a 'housewife's' benefit may find that the only way to get it is to underplay their abilities and emphasize what they cannot do. 'I think if the doctor or social worker had come into my home and it was dirty,' says one, 'they would have said I needed help. As it is, I don't think that they understand, any of them, what an effort it is to try. And what is the reward for trying?' Her application for the benefit was turned down. Another woman echoes her point: 'Anyone, however disabled, can modify their activities to be able to cope, as has been proved time and again. Praise is meted out very liberally to many disabled people who show determination and initiative to overcome their disability. But when it comes to housewives, they are penalized for trying to cope.'[4]

And along the way, anyone with a severe disability may, at any time, meet a helping professional who has decided views on how that coping is to be done. A social worker cites a colleague who would insist on cutting up her food for her because she lacked the use of one hand: 'She was unable to let herself be persuaded that my obvious rude health could only indicate that I had never found nourishing myself a problem!' A young woman dubbed mentally retarded, who has seen her share of social workers, finds that their version of caring is more like control:

> Social workers don't want to know the person, they're just doing it because it's a job. When they tell you to do this, that and the other, they don't take time to get to know you. 'You've got to listen to me' — just because they've been reading the books. But what that person has read might not be true at all. They don't know what they might do to a person's life — but what chance has that person got? When a person's life is all mixed up, the worst thing you can do is to say 'she's this, she's that and the other'. Just be prepared to listen. How can they suggest when they don't know the person or what the problem is?

They can, of course, because although they may not know the person, they know what the problem is *meant* to be, because they've been reading the books, and, come to that, writing them too, to define what the problem is. It is no coincidence, as the social scientists would be the first to point out, that ever since our Western societies first decided that 'special' professional services were needed for people with disabilities, the number of professional groups and individuals interested in them has grown, and with them, the number of people reckoned to need the 'special' services they provide. So there has been a growth in the number of people defined as 'blind' — although in Britain only some ten per cent of them are totally without sight. So there has been an increasing number of people, especially children, defined as 'mentally retarded' — although the vast majority of them have only a mild or 'borderline' degree of retardation. So in Britain, special schools for children with all sorts of disability have grown enormously since the Second World War. More and more people, in fact, have been defined as disabled enough to need 'special' services. It is a matter of commonsense rather than cynicism to point out

118

that the army of professional workers has an interest in keeping it that way.

They may need to make much of disability for professional reasons: they may elaborate theories on what disability 'means' and those theories may include the necessary presence of professional workers to help people 'come to terms' with their disability. They may need to make much of disability for financial reasons, feeding the public perception of 'helplessness' to elicit charitable funds. In 1980, a well known and highly professional British child care organization put a large advertisement in the newspapers headed: 'Colin will be eight years old for the rest of his life'. The story featured a lad who, we quickly learned, would *not* be dating any girls or looking for a job; even though he is in fact sixteen, he will be unlikely to add to the physical or mental capabilities of an eight-year-old; he will remain an 'unfortunate kid'; but if you send two pounds, it will buy a 'set of crayons and a colouring book to keep Colin busy'. No matter, perhaps, that his small abilities don't even get a mention. No matter, to the agency at least, that in their description of this young man who has spina bifida they are seriously misleading their readership by suggesting that this condition inevitably brings severe mental retardation − when in fact most young people who have it are of what is known as 'dull normal' intelligence. What matters is that the rest of us are assured not only that the Colins will be no threat to either our women or our jobs, but that there is a benevolent agency on hand whose work is absolutely essential in caring for them in their helplessness and that for a mere two pounds we can keep Colin colouring for the rest of his life, safely out of our way. Who knows, for two pounds more, we might even be able to catch a few more of them?

If professional workers need to make much of disability for reasons of status and seriousness, if their agencies may need to emphasize helplessness to underline what a good and necessary job they are doing, individual workers may also have their own reasons for doing the same. In his fascinating study *Power in the Helping Professions,* Adolf Guggenbuhl Craig shows how the shadow of the helping social worker is the controller, the shadow of the doctor the charlatan; he shows how professional

119

'helpers' need to establish the 'helplessness' of their customers to bolster their view of themselves. When sociologists, financial directors and Jungian analysts come to much the same conclusion, it is probably safe to say that professional 'helpers' have a problem.

But if they have a problem, it is people with disabilities who must live with it most closely. Just as in the institutions people tend to live up or down to the expectations of those with power, so will they if they meet the same expectations in other 'special' services. In his work on blindness, Robert Scott shows how professional workers construct different 'meanings' to the condition, according to the society in which they live and its own dominant approaches. So in the United States, blindness is seen predominantly in psychoanalytical terms, as a 'loss' to which people must learn to adjust, through the grief, shock and depression that it must bring. So in Italy and France, where work with blind people has traditionally been the preserve of the Catholic church, there is talk of the 'special' spirituality which this particular condition may bring in its wake. In England, where blind people are seen as particularly prone to depression and the doldrums, the goal of services is to cheer them along and help them to find good-natured responses to adversity. As Scott himself says, not too much should be made of these divisions. But he is nevertheless able to conclude that in the United States, at least, people conform to the predominant perception of the 'meaning' of blindness, and come through 'adjusted to their loss' and approved for that. We could add perhaps that too much British good nature brings its own dangers. It was at the end of 1979 that a travelling exhibitor of aids — and not one out for money — met within an hour two elderly women, both of when were defined as 'totally blind', who in fact could have been reading for some time if they had had the inexpensive gadget available to bolster partial sight and had their professional advisers even known of that gadget's existence.

That is one very obvious example of how people can be handicapped by professional perceptions of their disability. Others may be more subtle. But it is only commonsense to say that, if from childhood people grow up in families which have been told by doctors that 'nothing can be done', go to special schools which confirm 'differentness' and have their own low expectations, meet 'special' employment services which tell them they can't hope for much, and bump into professional helpers who have their own ideas of what disability must 'mean', then in the end those people stand more than a chance of believing the messages that they have so consistently been passed, by these interpreters of society. As one American disability rights activist says:

When people become disabled, they tend to think, because of society's attitudes: 'This is the way it's supposed to be. This must be the way I'm going to have to live. Now I'm disabled, I'm going to have to live differently than other people.' It's as though when they lose their legs, they lose their civil rights, and they think it's all part and parcel of the package. For example, someone who's a very involved person, a real gung-ho type, involved in all sorts of social changes. All of a sudden, he becomes disabled and he thinks, 'I'm helpless now. Now I'm supposed to accept my loss.'[5]

There must be another way. There is, and the clue to it is in the Swedish approach to blindness, as described by Robert Scott. There, he finds, blindness is seen above all as a technical problem, to be coped with by use of technical aids. As the workers say: 'Blindness does not mean that [blind persons'] other senses are blunted, that their personality has been blotted out or that the structure of the abilities that the individual has been equipped with has undergone a change.' This 'meaning' of blindness is very different from, say, the insistence on grief and mourning for loss that Scott sees in the United States. The reason may, to be sure, have something to do with Swedishness. But it may also have something to do with the fact that blind people in Sweden have insisted on running the blindness organizations themselves; they even got a law passed which says that no sighted person can hold executive office in one of these. The people who are 'professionals', in short, are the people who have been there themselves.

The approach is spreading. We have already seen something

of the programmes of help to which parents whose children have a severe disability may, if they're lucky, turn. The best of those programmes are the ones which recognize that it is parents who best know their own children, and which welcome parents as equal partners, rather than relegating them to a place where the professional workers tell them what to do. The same approach is blossoming in the self-help organizations which are slowly growing in England, organizations *of*, rather than *for*, people with disabilities. So the Spinal Injuries Association, for instance, has produced *So You're Paralysed*, an excellent basic guide to self-care, and its thick quarterly newsletter is filled with useful information on how to live more easily and fully with paralysis.

In the United States, there were reckoned to be no less than nine hundred self-help organizations for people with different disabilities by the end of the 1970s. The trend had found its coherence in the Alternative Living Movement — a potential revolution in the way that people with disabilities see themselves and so in the way that professional workers and others see them too. By the end of the decade, the journal *Archives of Physical Medicine and Rehabilitation* was hailing the movement as 'an idea whose time has come' and devoting a whole issue to its implications for the 'treatment' of physical disabilities.

What marks the movement out is that it is substantially consumer-controlled. It is the antithesis of the notion that people with disabilities are 'sick' or helpless; its leaders have particularly challenged the assumption that doctors should have a continuing control in their lives. The movement aims to help others with disabilities become responsible for living their own lives in their own way and to foster their fullest participation in the life of their community. It provides peer-counselling and helps people learn new skills; it offers advocacy and works to make the community more accessible in every way; sometimes it spawns opportunities for living arrangements as well. By the end of the 1970s, there were some sixty or seventy centres of the movement, of which the original Centre for Independent Living at Berkeley was the oldest established and best known. Most of the others were in academic communities too, for the movement has its limitations: it is still dominated by whites, although there is reckoned to be more disability among blacks; it is still primarily made up of young people, although the incidence of disability increases with age.

But the movement is well enough established to have attracted a promise of federal funds; and although the struggle to get that promise turned into hard cash was said to 'make Sisyphus look like a great achiever', although existing programmes are financially rocky, at least the movement is recognized as part of the official approach to severe physical disability. Some professional workers say: 'So what? We've been doing this all along.' Others see the movement as something to reckon with. 'In the past,' says one:

> professionals have had a limited view of the potentials of the severely disabled, and we have unfortunately defined limits for various disability categories . . . However, we have all seen exceptions to each one of these limitations. How many more exceptions would there be if we did not daily define such limitations? In fact, as professionals we need to help our patients define their expectations upward.

None of this is to say that people with disabilities don't need professional help; in fact, some times and in some places, they may need a sight more than they get at the moment. But it is to say that they and the professional workers together may need to take a look at the current cycle of expectation in which they are both caught and, as partners, start spiralling it up instead of down. It's then that the handicaps which overlay disability will start to peel away and that the barriers that people with disabilities may at the moment find in their search for housing, education, work and a fuller recognition of their rights will start to give way to opportunities. That's what we look at in the next section.

9

Housing

Jean Robinson moves round her kitchen to offer you a cup of tea with a delighted, deliberate pride. When you look over the apartment she shares with her friend Annie, she is at your elbow to point out each carefully dusted and placed ornament, each souvenir of good times past. When she phones you up, there's usually some news to share about what she's been up to – visiting friends in the neighbourhood, learning to cook another dish, mastering public transport on her own. Jean Robinson is at home, and it shows in her every activity.

There have been times enough over her forty-odd years when she wondered whether she ever would be. Polio at the age of three took her into a series of hospitals and boarding schools; an unwelcoming society sent her at seventeen into a large, distant mental retardation institution. 'It was terrible, horrible,' she remembers now. 'There were bars at the windows; it's still like that now, you know.' But there she stayed for twenty-five years, until a place came up in a rehabilitation ward and a nurse there helped her move out into a hostel. 'It was strange after being in a big place, you know, having my own room. I'd make my bed, go out shopping when I wanted to – in the hospital, we used to have to have a nurse with us when we went out.' Then the chance came up of leaving the hostel for this apartment, with Annie who had clocked up even more years in hospital than she had. There was some hesitation: 'But you have to give things a try, don't you? You can't give up easy, can you?'

So in she moved, and she's got too much to enjoy now to spend time looking back. She pleases herself as to when she comes in and out and whom she invites; she likes her nice soft bed after the one at the hostel. On one thing she is absolutely clear. She never, at any time has wanted to go back to the hospital. 'No, I'm glad I'm out. Twenty-five years of it, you've had it. It's a long time, isn't it?' It was a long wait. But Jean Robinson knows now what it is to have a home.

A house is more than four walls which hold up a roof and enclose a variety of functional spaces. For all of us, it is the basis of our security and our exploration of the world. It is the place where we find our privacy, express our personality and preferences and experiment with change. It is the place where we build and enjoy and battle over the close relationships we have chosen to make. It is the place from which we go out to tackle the world, at the centre of a whole range of other relationships — with shopkeepers, neighbours and friends — which bring security in their familarity. It is the place we come back to for comfort, reassurance and a recharging of the batteries. It is the place into whose familiar contours we can flop and relax and be ourselves. And if it isn't any or all of these things, then we would like it to be.

The vast majority of people who have disabilities live in ordinary housing. And that may present them with extra-ordinary difficulties, for ordinary housing is rarely constructed with their possible quirks in mind. So even moving about her own home takes an enormous amount of discipline for one woman who walks with difficulty, on the days she walks at all.

You cannot say 'I'll leave chores until tomorrow and do twice as much then' You haven't the energy. Everything takes longer. If you've forgotten something in another room, either you have to depend on someone else to get it for you, waste precious energy getting it yourself or do without. You cannot stop thinking about and concentrating on yourself and your environment.

She knows that she is lucky: the family could afford to install a lift and maintain it, so at least she can get upstairs in her own place. Others are not so fortunate. So the family of a boy with severe mental and physical disabilities has to work out a way of meeting his and their needs in their none-too-large publicly provided house. It used to be easy enough to carry him upstairs to bed, but now he is approaching adolescence, he is getting heavy to lift; and soon he will have to rely on his father, who is a shift-worker. There is no physical reason why a lift shouldn't be installed. But the public help available for such adaptations will not cover the full cost, and the family simply can't afford to make it up.

Very many other people with disabilities will also have found that their house doesn't work for them. It's not simply that it isn't adapted to their needs. They are also more likely than others to live in housing which would be inconvenient for anyone, let alone someone with a disability. By the end of the 1960s, it's been reckoned, people in Britain who had some incapacity were more, not less likely than people who did not, to live in a house which lacked the basic amenities of indoor lavatory, sink with tap, bath and cooker. And that is not just because disability increases with age, and elderly people in Britain can reckon to have worse housing than the rest of the population. The deprivation that comes with lack of amenities runs right through the age range. An official Government survey, made at about the same time, found that no less than 800,000 households could either do with rehousing or with substantial alterations to the place they were in because that place posed such problems to their members with physical disabilities. A quarter of these households had to make do without an inside lavatory — and had members who were, according to the survey's standards, very severely, severely, or appreciably handicapped. For no less than 150,000 people, parts of their own home were inaccessible. That could mean, for instance, years of sleeping in the living room for the person with a disability.

The first reaction to these appalling figures was to look to the building of new, 'special' housing, suitable for people who use wheelchairs indoors, usually clustered together and sometimes with a 'warden' or helper on call. For one elderly couple, both severely disabled by arthritis, a purpose-built bungalow in a cluster of this sort has brought new happiness. They have nothing but praise for the people who make it possible for them to go on living in their own place, when he is eighty and can walk only a few yards with elbow crutches and she is seventy-one, can walk about fifty yards with the aid of a spinal brace and is resisting the doctor's suggestion that she should take to a wheelchair. 'It is wonderful,' she says, 'what one can do if one is determined enough!' The local authority has built a workshop in the garden, where her husband does woodwork and makes tools to help them in the house, and converted their bathroom to take a shower. She continues to serve on different committees and take an active part in the life of their town. There is intercom contact with the warden of the scheme, should they need her; the district nurse comes once a fortnight and the home help for two hours twice a week; the doctor looks in every month and so does the chiropodist.

A widow of seventy-two, who also has severe arthritis, has not been so fortunate in her move to a 'special' flat after forty years in her own home. 'I did not know it was possible for anyone to be so unhappy inwardly. I have always been told that I was a very happy person. I could always conceal my pain, I have really done everything I can to keep my independence. I feel so discouraged now.' Her electric wheelchair used to enable her to move about the community; she used to go to the theatre, to church, to the debating society and adult education classes; she used to visit her friends and use the mobile library. She was told when she moved to the flat that the kerbs would be flattened and ramps put in. This has not yet happened — and that, in housing designed especially for people with severe disabilities! Because building work has been going on around the flats, the chair got constant punctures. She has now given it up because she simply cannot afford the repairs. So she is housebound. The voluntary worker who visits the flats just says: 'You're not the only one, you must accept the fact that you are disabled.' She was assured when she first looked at the flat that the automatic washing machine she has to use would fit it. So it does, but the pressure in the hot water tap is too low, so she must fill it with cold — and that puts up the cost of using the machine. She has little privacy — the warden of the cluster will walk in without warning. She feels despairing. 'When I think my future will be just sitting in four walls waiting for death, I wish I had never moved into this flat.'

Many other people with disabilities will not get the chance to find out whether this sort of sheltered housing suits them or not. For them 'home' will be one of the variety of residential institutions. People whose physical disability is severe enough to require intimate personal help will be counted 'too disabled' for sheltered housing. If family arrangements break down, or if they want to take the normal step, as a young adult, of establishing their own life in their own place, instead of living on the fringes of their parents' lives, that place will most usually be a room, or a bit of it, in a residential home or even a hospital unit. We have seen how very far from any concept of an ordinary 'home life' the regimes in these places may be. We can add that their siting – on the fringes of hospital grounds, in converted mansions – may confirm their distance from ordinary patterns of everyday life in ordinary streets. For some people, they may offer fulfilment. For others, like the members of the British Union of the Physically Impaired Against Segregation, they are anathema: 'Disabled people's general position as an oppressed group is seen most clearly in residential institutions, where isolation and segregation have been carried to extremes. Despite the efforts of staff and volunteers, segregated institutions remain prison-like scrapheaps of this society.'

People who are mentally retarded may get their first taste of institutional living early; we have seen how hospital wards offer the antithesis of a home life for the extremely vulnerable children who must live in them. Others, older and less severely disabled, will, if they are lucky, be able to move into a community home or hostel. But they will rarely get that chance as part of the normal process of growing up and establishing their own life. Most usually, the offer will come only when their parents are too tired and frail to care for them any longer, or even only when one parent dies. The offer may not come at all. Then the only alternative for them, as it is already for the people counted 'too retarded' to cope with life in a community hostel, will be a bed in the ward of an institution, than which nothing could be less like an ordinary house, either physically or in the opportunities it offers. 'What will happen when I can't care any longer?' is still the most agonizing question that

128

parents have to face, and none the less so for the fact that society has already provided them with an answer that few want to have to contemplate, let alone accept. As one mother of a very severely disabled son says: 'Why can't we face the fact that there is no purpose in keeping them alive if all we can do is shut them up in institutions with each other? Of course I should mourn if I lost him — but I would rather he died a natural death in his teens than be left somewhere to vegetate.'

What to do? The most usual answers, developed now over some years in most Western societies, have to do with the notion of a progression — from ordinary housing adapted as necessary, to sheltered clusters, to institutions 'in the community' which offer twenty-four-hour care for people whose disabilities are less severe, to institutions further from it and often with a medical tinge, which offer the same twenty-four-hour care for people with very severe disabilities. The balance between these provisions may be altered from place to place and time to time. So by the end of the 1970s, there was a special Office of Independent Living in the United States' Department of Housing and Urban Development, pledged to devote five per cent of the department's funds to barrier-free housing; a special project at the end of the decade reserved $99 million for over 3,000 housing units for people with disabilities including those with mental illnesses. Programmes like this run alongside the other sorts of provision which make up the basic pattern, in the United States as elsewhere. So in Britain, the effort has been to provide more and better of all the pattern's components. Local authorities have had a duty, over a decade, to help people with physical disabilities with the cost of adapting their ordinary housing. They have been urged to build more special and often clustered housing, and some voluntary housing schemes have even tried to 'desegregate' this sort of housing by offering 'mixed' schemes that reserve a fixed proportion of their units to people with disabilities. Local authority and private and voluntary agencies have provided special homes for younger people with physical disabilities, so that they do not have to end up in hospital provision; at the same time, that special hospital provision has itself grown.

This basic pattern of progression has been echoed for people who are mentally retarded, in Britain and most other Western countries as well. There are unstaffed apartments and group homes, supported by visiting staff as necessary. There are staffed residential homes 'in the community', set up mostly to cater for people with moderate degrees of retardation. And then there are large and relatively distant institutions for people who are more severely disabled, which may offer a high standard of physical amenity and be called 'central residential homes' in Scandinavia, or environments which range from the appalling to the cleanly clinical in the USA and Britain, and be called 'State Developmental Center' or 'mental handicap hospital'. So the pattern is clear: people should progress, according to the degree of their disability and the personal resources they can call on, from ordinary housing to something which is not, recognizably, housing at all, but is deemed necessary because it meets their 'special needs'.

There are just two snags to this approach. The first is that what looks like an orderly progression to planners seldom turns out that way in practice. So although the number of housing adaptations in Britain has rocketed — from 28,000 in 1973 to 60,000 in 1978 — most of these were very minor, and the different means tests imposed have meant that many people have not been able to afford the major adaptations that would really make a difference to the way they live. There is not enough sheltered housing, either, and that there is, is not being properly used. For a start, many people who could qualify prefer not to uproot themselves from the patterns of friendship that they have established in their own neighbourhoods over the years — and who can question the wisdom of that decision? Even if they do move, they may wish they hadn't because they would rather live in an ordinary street with a mixture of neighbours than in a 'disabled ghetto' — especially if they are younger. Even if they are willing to move, they may not know what opportunities are on offer; one study in London showed almost complete confusion about what special housing was available among the staff of the responsible authorities, let alone among prospective tenants. Even if people have to move from their family homes, the promised options may not be available: community alternatives to traditional institutions may be in desperately short supply, especially for people whose disabilities are severe. Many people, in short, are still in housing that doesn't meet their needs, and many others are still living in institutions which cannot qualify as housing at all.

The second snag to this 'progression' approach is more fundamental, and would still be there however efficiently the system was run and however much money was available to expand it. What the approach assumes is that people whose disabilities are severe can't live in ordinary housing but must, in the end, when they are no longer cared for by their families, end up in one sort of institutional setting or another. It assumes that the very people who have need of easiest access to their local communities are the ones condemned to live on their fringes. There must be another way.

There is, and it is working in all the schemes which recognize that the assertion that people with severe disabilities cannot live in ordinary housing once they have to leave the ordinary housing in which they have been living is as ridiculous as it sounds. It is working in all the schemes which separate the need for *housing*, which is common to us all, from the need for *care*, which different people will need in different concentrations at different times, instead of blending the two in a package called 'residential care' which certainly doesn't offer ordinary housing and may offer far more care than people actually need. It is working in the schemes which take as their starting-point that people in our Western societies live in houses, among others whose mixture of abilities and inabilities is different from their own, and then take care to those houses, rather than assuming that people who need care should up sticks and move to a place where it is dispensed.

Both the Danish Collective Houses and the Swedish Fokus system have shown that it is perfectly possible to deliver the personal attention that people with severe physical disabilities may need outside institutional settings. Both are based on apartments in 'mixed' blocks, with some communal facilities and personal assistance laid on, and they cater for people whose disabilities are every bit as severe as those of others who end up in residential homes and hospital units elsewhere. What neither approach has yet completely cracked is the question of over-concentration. In *Designing for the Disabled*, Selwyn Goldsmith points out that the Danish Collective Houses, which offer a third of their tenancies to people with severe disabilities, are hardly the 'integrated' living places that their designers may have hoped for; there is a clear division between the 'able-bodied' and 'disabled' tenants. He finds the Fokus schemes succeed better, although here again, there is little mixing between the two sets of tenants, especially as the communal facilities are used by the tenants with disabilities only.

To some people who don't have the option of this kind of independent living, the question of concentration may not matter at all. To others it may. They may wish to live in an ordinary street, among people who do not share their range of disabilities. It is an ordinary enough aspiration. But for it to be met, two things are needed: far more housing that is fit for people with physical disabilities to live in, and a flexible system of travelling care attendants.

Adapted housing may mean existing stock that is converted. It may also mean new housing in ordinary settings which is automatically made convenient for people with a whole range of physical abilities and disabilities, rather than 'special' housing, often clustered together. In Britain, it is called 'mobility housing', and what it does is extend the range of normal provision to encompass special needs. It has been reckoned that as many as ninety-six per cent of the people categorized as having physical problems – including up to half those who use wheelchairs – could live in it comfortably. That also means, of course, that it is comfortable for people who aren't categorized as having disabilities at all. It is the direction for the future and we need far more of it.

The second essential element in ensuring that everyone who chooses to live in ordinary housing can, irrespective of their degree of disability, we are much slower to provide. There are the beginnings in the care attendant schemes in the USA, which have come in the wake of the Independent Living Movement. There are the beginnings in the Department of Housing and

Urban Development's projects for the delivery of meals, personal assistance and 'chore services' to people with disabilities in subsidized housing. In Britain, where in theory at least there have been 'meals on wheels', district nursing and home help services available from local authorities for many years, people are beginning to go further than that. We have already seen, in 'Family Matters', the huge difference that the flexible Crossroads care attendant scheme is making to the people it serves. If this service was extended to single people who now must often, for want of support, live in institutions, then they too could exchange the assurance of help that they don't need during twenty-four hours a day, for the assurance of the individually-planned help they do need at critical times. Then they could get on with their own lives in their own way. That is a path for the future, and we need more schemes which enable people to take it.

None of this supposes that residential homes will close. For some people, this option will still be the one that suits them best. Some will choose a home which does not make too many demands on them. Others will hope to find one which is run on the assumption that they will take as full a responsibility as possible for their own lives. They will seek a home which insists, for instance, on their choosing, budgeting for and directing the preparation of their own food; which expects a communal responsibility in running the place, through meetings between staff and residents; which sees the staff as an essential adjunct to the mechanical aids that people may use to bolster their own independence, performing essential tasks that the residents cannot manage, but at a time and in a way that the residents themselves decide as individuals.

None of this supposes, either, an end to the different personal and highly individualistic solutions that people with severe physical disabilities may build for themselves — indeed, it should, by denting the expectation of 'inevitable' progression to the institution, actually encourage these initiatives. So, for instance, one man who has always had very severe disabilities as the result of cerebral palsy, who cannot speak and is confined to a wheelchair, is something of an expert on housing, running from his own house, an advisory service for people in need.

The house itself he fills with people who urgently need a place to live, as well as full-time helpers; the community is made up of about twelve people at any one time. Some of the other members of it — and they range from political refugees, a young woman who is in despair about her approaching blindness and a mother who is trying to rebuild her life after losing custody of her two children, to a woman who has known her share of psychiatric troubles — will sometimes provide the help he needs as well.

> This means that in my house there is almost a small community, some of whom I depend on to help but who in turn also want my assistance in giving them a place to live. This interdependence is very healthy, because there is nothing quite as corrupting for all concerned as being completely dependent on too few people. This also tends to exhaust the helpers, who feel under too much strain, and can lead to various kinds of abuse. One advantage of a very mixed community ... is the reality that if someone happens to become overstressed and starts to ill-treat the disabled person, or the latter exploits overmuch the helper, there are enough people about to be aware of what is going on and to exert community pressure. . . I can promise you, there are few less pleasant things than to be cared for by someone who is constantly over-tired and under too much strain. This makes life tense, unpleasant and unfulfilled.

He knows that his sort of community living won't suit all the people with severe disabilities all the time. But he wishes that more had the opportunity to try it, either through finding a guarantor for a mortage from an association concerned with disability or through a housing association which can, in Britain, acquire property and let it at subsidized rents.[1]

What this and the other housing solutions for people with severe physical disabilities do is the very opposite of laying down the sort of pattern they so often find they must conform to now. It simply acknowledges that enabling people to lead 'as normal a life as possible' must start from offering them a place that they can really call 'home' as the basis of their security and their exploration.

What is true for people with severe physical disabilities is no less true for people who have severe mental retardation. For them, in fact, a model of a housing service has already been running successfully for over a decade. The Eastern Nebraska Community Office of Retardation in the United States grasped very early on in its life that it is possible to separate people's need for *housing*, which is common to us all, from their need for *care*, which will vary with the degree of their disability. When ENCOR set up shop, there were forty-two people from its region waiting to go into the distant and dreadful State institution; a decade later, there were none, because ENCOR had provided alternatives, and some 260 people had come home to their own region from that institution as well. And what they had come home to was not a small, local residential institution, but a house – and not even a standard type of house, 'fit' for people who are mentally retarded, but a whole range of opportunities for living. ENCOR offers people housing for a start, and then it offers them the individual, planned and specific degree of personal help and services they need to enable them to live there enjoyably and with fulfilment. So, by 1977, in a total population of not much over half a million, 110 adults were living in ENCOR's sixty-four 'alternative living units' – alone, sharing with the partner of their choice, with friends, or with ENCOR staff; fifty-three children were living in thirty-two different settings, either with what the British would call professional foster parents, or with ENCOR staff. This agency doesn't need 'special care wards' for children who can no longer live with their own families; it has found out that one highly specialist unit for five children, on a temporary basis, is all that's needed to give them the help they need to move on to a more 'normal' setting. It doesn't need to concentrate together the children with severe disturbances of behaviour either; it has closed down the special unit it had for them and now offers them often intensive support in ordinary, individualized settings. It would prove the same for the most profoundly disabled minority of adults, too, and the most severely disturbed, if it only had the funds to do so. ENCOR reckons that within its alternative living units, backed by its seven small 'training residences' for children and seven for adults, it could,

135

given the chance and the funds to hire the number of staff it needs, offer a home to anyone who needs one.

The beauty of ENCOR, in the end, is the beauty of Crossroads. Both offer people the help they need, as individuals, in a place that all of us would recognize as 'normal', rather than forcing them to accept a package marked 'residential care' of which they may need only fragments. What ENCOR has put together others know about in parts. In Britain, Parents for Children is echoing experience in different parts of the United States by finding adoptive parents for children with often severe disabilities, physical and mental. For a decade, the North-west of England division of Barnardo's has been welcoming children with often the same degree of disability into its 'ordinary' children's homes, to the delight and growth of staff and children alike; it has also pioneered the ENCOR concept of 'alternative living units' backed by a 'core residence' for children who would otherwise be candidates for a traditional institution.

Adults who are mentally retarded are living alone, or in small households or with partners of their choice. Many agencies in many places have built on the pioneering work in Sweden which showed that they may need far less support than was originally thought, provided that that support is sensitive and flexible. People who are mentally retarded are sharing tenancies with people who are not, whether these are students or ordinary workers. People are getting together to share their lives across the boundaries imposed by IQ tests in communities like the fifty set up by l'Arche across the world from downtown Chicago to inner-city Liverpool to rural Ontario to central Calcutta, and beyond. People whose retardation is very severe are beginning to get their chance: the Wessex hostels in England have been showing for a decade that they are more likely to get the specialist help they need in local community settings than in traditional large institutions.

When the official Jay Committee, set up by the British Government to look at the nursing and care offered to mentally retarded children and adults reported in 1979, it came up with a 'model of care' which drew on the best of what was happening to explode the notion that the large, traditional institutions which squat all over our Western societies are needed at all. In its vision of the future, every person who is mentally retarded, whatever his or her degree of disability, could go on living in the ordinary community, with the individual support needed to make this possible. It called its model 'unashamedly ideal-istic'. But its components are there already, in different parts of the world. What it takes to start bringing them together is what we all recognize as the basis of our Western lives: an ordinary house in an ordinary street, a place from which we can explore and a place to which we can come home, and feel welcome.

10

Education

A group of children with severe learning difficulties are talking about the way life seems. They say they are teased by the others in the neighbourhood while they wait for their special school bus — 'they know it, you see, well, you can't miss it, can you?' 'I'm not allowed to play out at home,' says one, 'because I go to this school and the kids know that this school is for mental handicaps.' They wish they could go to a 'proper' school.[1]

A young man with cerebral palsy who went to a special boarding school between the ages of ten and twelve remembers: 'When I left I was very self-conscious in normal society, having been in a small, enclosed group of unnormal children.' He made no friends at the regular school he then went to, or indeed for some years afterwards. 'From eighteen to twenty-two I studied people as I would ducks in the park. I had no contribution to make.'

A mother, concerned at the standard of education her son is getting in his special school, applied to several private ones in the hope of a place for him. All but one refused without even meeting the boy, because he goes about in a wheelchair. One headmaster said he thought it was 'unreasonable' to expect normal children to accept ones with disabilities.

Teachers in the United States could, by 1980, buy a puppet kit called the 'Kids on the Block', designed to teach children who have no defined disabilities about children who do, in a 'non-threatening and un-preachy fashion' and to show that the two groups can be friends. Some of the puppets have disabilities, others do not. One conversation between them starts with a 'normal' puppet saying: 'Gee, Mark, I don't know if I should play with you. What if I catch cerebral palsy? My mom would be really mad!'

Whatever else we do or don't get out of our education, our school is the place where we learn our first lessons about the society we live in beyond the family. We make friends and visit their houses, and meet parents who are not our own. We meet other children who are more or less clever than we are, more or less good at all sorts of things. We learn something of that continuum of ability and inability that makes up our human societies and something of where we are on it.

Children with disabilities who go to special schools will learn the same lessons, but the message they pick up may be very different. They will learn that the world of the majority is not for them, that they are 'special' and separate, that they are supposed to have more in common with children who share their disability than others, simply because they share that disability. They will learn, as they wait for the school bus that takes them out of their neighbourhood, that they are supposed to have a different relationship with that neighbourhood from everyone else. They will learn that meeting your friends out of school is a complicated business, because they are scattered all over town; if they go to a boarding school they will — as 'normal' children in boarding schools also do — learn that lesson harder.

As they get older, society's assurance that they should lead 'as normal a life as possible' may sit pretty uneasily with their experience of it so far. At the limit, they will have little notion of what that rubric means, because they have had little chance to find out their own place on the continuum of ability and inability; what they will know, first and foremost, is that they are among 'the disabled'. They will, in short, be extremely handicapped in their relationships with the 'normal' world when they leave their small, 'special' one. There is research to back commonsense: children who have been to special schools are more likely to devalue themselves than others with disabilities who have not; young children who go to special units in ordinary schools are more likely to make friends outside their class than children in special schools.

The handicap isn't just theirs. Children who go to ordinary

schools will also have learnt that there is an 'inevitable' cut-off between them and some others, that the 'spastics' and the 'dumdums' who go off in their special bus have little in common with them at all; they will see the disability because they have had little chance to get to know the person. Just as children in special schools will have learned that they can expect to live on the fringe of the ordinary world, so the others will have learned that there is a 'norm' which excludes. The adults may try to bridge the gap with puppet shows or, in other places, special kits and projects. They may encourage their students to write off to specialist organizations which deal with 'the mentally retarded' or 'the disabled' to ask for information about them. They will build their bridges gingerly, because they too are handicapped by their own past schooling. It may not, perhaps, even occur to them that the best way to learn about people is to spend time with them, find out what you have in common and what you don't, learn to see each other as individuals and not simply as representatives of a group to whom you may have been told to 'be kind' or of whom you are a little frightened. So 'ordinary' children too grow up handicapped in their understanding, learning the lessons that their adults learned before them, and the segregation of the institution may come to seem as normal to them as the segregation of the school bus. And the slogans about 'integrating the disabled' may get to sound peculiar, and even as 'unreasonable' to them as they did to that headmaster.

But if the handicap is a mutual one, it is the children who go to special schools who must bear the brunt of it. And more and more of them, in Britain at least, have been growing up with it. Although the 1944 Education Act, on which the school system is founded, lays down that whenever possible children should find their education within the ordinary system, the numbers in special schools have rocketed — from about 50,000 in 1949 to 135,000 at the end of the 1970s, with no less than eleven categories of child to fit into nineteen categories of school.[2] The figures were certainly boosted by some 20,000 at the beginning of the decade, when children with severe learning difficulties were brought for the first time into the educational system. But even so, the message is clear: more and more children are being defined as unable to 'fit' into 'normal' patterns and expectations.

This could mean, of course, that we have become a great deal more sophisticated in our definitions of individual need. But does it? Far and away the fastest growth areas in the special school system have been in provision for children officially dubbed 'educationally subnormal (moderate)' — those with moderate learning difficulties — and 'maladjusted' — which, in the words of one official report, seems to mean only that they 'find it difficult to accept the normal framework of life and work in schools'.

Yet we could say that every child, and each of us, has grown up with areas of difficulty in learning. The use of IQ tests to mark the cut-off between children who can have these in ordinary schools and children who must have them in special ones has been increasingly challenged in recent years; critics would say that the overwhelming over-representation of black and working class children in ESN(M) schools simply shows that tests designed to white, middle-class norms are singularly ill-equipped to measure their abilities. Definitions made on this basis can be random: one recent British study showed that young people leaving ESN(M) boarding schools had much the same range of intelligence and difficulties in learning social survival skills as young people from any other juvenile institution. The questions around IQ testing are international. In 1980, a California court ruled that it should no longer be allowed as the basis of educational placement.

If we all grow up with areas of learning difficulty, we could all say too that we have grown up with some degree of difficulty in accepting the normal framework of life and work in school; we may even pride ourselves on that in later years. At what point do we become officially 'maladjusted'? The answer seems to be: when the school authority decides we are. At the end of the 1970s, the 'incidence' of maladjustment was ten times higher in one part of London than in another, and the 'need' for special units for students with disturbed behaviour varied greatly across England; there seemed to be little objective definition of 'maladjustment' at all.

This would be less alarming, perhaps, if once defined as

141

maladjusted, students were offered programmes clearly tailored to their individual needs. But an official Government survey of the 'behavioural units' which had mushroomed to cater for some 4,000 British children by 1977, shows that this doesn't necessarily happen at all. There was little in the organization of the units to confirm that their inhabitants were valued members of the school population. Funding was *ad hoc*; the units were in a variety of old houses, disused schools and huts − including one building where the only running water was what came through the ceiling. Uncertain funding meant a lack of coherent programmes. Age-groups were sometimes mixed, the staff got little guidance and only a limited number of academic subjects could be taught. 'In general,' the Government's inspectors found, 'teachers in units were more vague about the arrangements for return to normal schooling than they were about admission to the units.' Criteria for completing a course ranged from showing 'improved behaviour and willingness to learn' to 'ability to assure the school that the pupil intends to work', to goals that were at least measurable, like 'completion of five consecutive days' satisfactory work and behaviour'. But it was possible, in theory at least, for children to remain in some of these units throughout their educational career.

The questions raised by these definitions and outcomes run across the whole of special schooling. What are 'special educational needs' and how should they be met? The British Warnock Committee which took the first official look at the system for ninety years in its 1978 report, reckoned that the proportion of children with special educational needs was not limited to the two per cent in special schools, but included twenty per cent of the entire school population. But if the large majority of special needs can be met in ordinary schools, why can't the minority as well? Whatever else they provide, the special schools offer the certainty of social handicap and, as we have seen, a sometimes damagingly low cycle of expectation. What are the advantages to outweigh these disadvantages? What is essential in the provision that cannot be created elsewhere?

The questions are not just for those children and parents

who use special schools today and those who may use them tomorrow. They are questions for us all, for the shape of our schooling systems has something to say about the shape of our societies as a whole. A country which relies heavily on special, segregated schools is a country which is drawing the boundaries of its 'norm' more tightly and more closely; it is a country which, for all it may pride itself on an ostensible pluralism and tolerance, is actually making more and more demands on its citizens to conform to a certain pattern of behaviour and competence. A country which is trying to construct a school system which extends the bounds of the 'normal' to encompass those children it has hitherto excluded is a country which is trying to extend the bounds of its more general tolerance. Which way do we want our societies to go?

In Britain, by 1980, the question was unanswered. There was a Government intention to redefine the whole scope of special education along the lines that the Warnock report had recommended. The rigid categories of children and of schools were on their way out; instead, some of the old terms were to be changed and others used merely as a description of convenience, with the idea that this would lead to greater flexibility in placement and bring regular schools and special ones closer together.

But the essential question, of whether some educational needs could *only* be met in special schools, was fudged. As Warnock had done before it, the Government saw scope for bringing more children with disabilities into the regular school system. In future, it proposed, those defined as having special educational needs would be educated alongside the rest if the arrangements made were capable of meeting those needs, compatible with the efficient education of the majority and with efficient use of public resources, and took 'proper account' of the wishes of the parents. Just where children would spend their schooldays, in short, would continue to have more to do with administrative and financial convenience than it would with their individual needs. And that, the Government was sure, as Warnock had been sure before it, meant that there would always be a need — albeit unspecific and undefined — for special schools.

But will there? It is a good decade now since the Scandinavian countries first planned to bring as many children with physical disabilities as possible into their regular school systems.

In 1970, Anders was ten and went to a regular school in his home town in Sweden. He had severe muscular dystrophy and spent all his time in a wheelchair; he had no access problems, however, because the school was built to accommodate wheelchairs and their occupants. His doctor was against his going to a regular school; the head was at first dubious. But it worked. Anders had a full-time care assistant, an electric typewriter and a specially-adapted desk. He left school an hour early because he got tired; he had physiotherapy once a week after school at a local clinic; he got to and from school and the clinic in a community minibus. He kept up well with his schoolwork because he could study what he had missed during PE lessons. He was one of the leaders of his class and had many friends who visited him at home, just as he went out with and visited them in his own electric 'car'. The head found it 'quite natural' for him to be in the school, despite his very severe disabilities.

In 1970 Marit was in her first year at a Norwegian university; together with other children with cerebral palsy, she started her school life in a special school and, like them, she had got very bored of the lack of demands there and longed to leave. When she was thirteen, she transferred to a regular school. She didn't find the problems of coping with an old, unadapted building overwhelming at all; she had always found people ready to carry her wheelchair up and down stairs. She had been in small classes as well as larger ones and found that the supposed advantages of the first for children with disabilities didn't really exist. She had never had a special assistant; fellow students and teachers always pitched in when she needed help, and ordinary teachers were just as understanding as those in her special school. She had never been teased: 'Children', she said, 'are not as cruel as adults seem to think.' She was grateful to the special school teachers she'd had, and thought that a spell in a special school had probably been a good idea; but she also thought they had tended to over-protect her and that she could have made the transition earlier.

The difference between the British approach to integrating

children with severe physical disabilities into regular schools and the Scandinavian one is that the first calls it 'experimental' and the second the norm. But by the mid 1970s, Anderson and Cope, in their study of British schemes, were able to conclude that no child who fell within the normal range of intelligence but had a physical disability should go to a special school at all. They found that children in special units in primary schools achieve just as much educationally as those in special schools. They found the first group had a wider circle of friends and that children who have not yet learned to live down to adult expectations simply don't discriminate against or tease others who are 'special'. (As one young Swede with very severe disabilities as a result of cerebral palsy said: 'Why should they? There's nothing wrong with them.') They found that parents got just as much support from regular teachers as they did from special ones; they found that regular teachers welcomed the arrangement.

When they turned to students with severe physical disabilities in secondary schools, they found again that they were doing just as well as, if not better than, they had done in the special schools from which they came. They found that none of them wanted to go back, that only four out of fifty-seven even mentioned teasing as a problem. They were able to conclude that at this age, students should be not in special units at all, but in regular classes.

Making ordinary schools fit for special needs can take a variety of forms. There can be full integration in regular classes, with special help as needed, time in regular classes with 'resource centres' to turn to for special programmes of help. There can be time spent in a special unit, with maximum integration, individually planned, into the regular programme. One way and another, these options should be able to cater for a very wide range of needs indeed, including those for special technology, as American schools have found out in their successful integration into the regular system of about three-quarters of all children who are blind. The National Federation of the Blind in Britain sees no reason why a system of special units and peripatetic teachers cannot be set up in that country; they can point to the arrangements in one Liverpool school which has pioneered the approach. A woman who is now twenty-eight looks back on her schooldays in a special boarding school for blind girls.

I learnt to read braille, do geometry in braille, and mostly academic things, except for deportment, which was, in fact, a skill we needed to learn. But practical things such as cooking, using make-up and even mobility were hardly covered at all. I think I could have learned those things with specialist help in an ordinary school. As it was, most of us were completely ignorant and unprepared for what the outside world was going to be like, particularly in terms of the attitudes we were likely to encounter.

If ordinary schools can be made fit for children who often have highly specialized technical needs, they can be made fit too for children who have severe learning difficulties. The few British experiments in providing special units for them in regular schools, with maximum individual integration into regular classes, have shown, once again, that their abilities if anything increase compared to those of children in special schools, that they are not teased or ostracized by other children if the behaviour of teachers eliminates this option. The Eastern Nebraska Community Office of Retardation has shown the thoroughgoing integrated future. It has managed to close every one of its special schools, integrating even children with severe disturbances of behaviour into regular ones, by providing specialist teachers to help staff special units and encourage maximum individual integration.

So there is nothing at all to say that regular schools cannot be made fit for children with special educational needs. What Britain lacks is a commitment to making sure that they do, a framework to ensure that what is now 'experiment' becomes the normal approach to providing special education. The United States seems to have found both that commitment and that framework.

The base from which the two countries started was very different. By the beginning of the 1970s, when children with severe learning difficulties were finally brought, by law, into the English educational system, similar children in the USA were still excluded from education altogether, as were many others because of their problems of behaviour. 'Special' education, for American children with learning difficulties at least, was more often provided in classes attached to ordinary schools than in special schools, and those classes were too often dumping-grounds rather than constructive places of learning. But in 1976, when England passed an Education Act which confirmed the rule of administrative convenience by including a clause saying special education should be provided in ordinary schools unless this was 'impracticable', 'incompatible with the provision of efficient instruction in the schools' or would involve 'unreasonable public expenditure', the United States took a very different route. And while the 1976 Education Act has now been dropped, the 1976 Education of All Handicapped Children Act remains to bring all those it covers the right to a free and appropriate public education, within a general notion that twelve per cent of the total school population has special educational needs.

This legislation contrasts sharply with what the Government promised in 1980 for England and Wales. For a start, it has a philosophy behind it which has to do with more than pragmatism. It puts the burden of proof that children need to be removed from the mainstream of education firmly on the authorities which would remove them. Rather than expecting children to fit tidily into regular patterns or else pay the price in exclusion from those patterns, it encourages their adaptation to the needs of the children they serve, and the placement for each child must be the least restrictive, the most 'normal' one possible.

The philosophy has practical backing. While in England, the Government made it clear that local education authorities would have to cope with the extra expense of adapting ordinary education as best they could, and that in a situation of severe restraint on all public expenditure, the American law tackles the financial disincentives to integrated education. States are obliged to refund school districts for the extra costs of adapting ordinary schools and curricula, with Federal financial support due to hit its ceiling of forty per cent by 1982.

The interests of individual children are also far more carefully safeguarded under the American law than is proposed in England. Warnock saw little need to question the power of professional workers. Although it included in its report an entire chapter headed 'Parents as Partners', it offered them no place in the assessment of their child. The Government's own proposals took their tone from Warnock. Parents were to have no access at all to professional documents that relate to their child – unlike parents in the USA, who have an absolute right to see all the professional reports and tests on which a proposed special educational placement is based. If English parents didn't like the proposed placement, they would be able to appeal to a committee whose decisions, when it came to 'special' children, would not be binding on the educational authority; beyond that, they would only be able to make the cumbersome appeal to the Secretary of State, which the experience of years had shown to be rarely successful. If American parents don't like the proposed placement, by contrast, they have a right to contest it within twenty to forty-five days of requesting a hearing. When they come before the State Commissioner of Education, at a time and place convenient to them, they have the right to be legally represented, to bring their own expert witnesses and to have all the records which relate to their child. If they still disagree with the decision, they have a right of appeal.

The contrasts continue once the child has been assessed and placed. In England under the Government's proposals, education authorities would have the right to tell parents that their request for a multi-disciplinary reassessment was 'unreasonable' and the duty only to inform them, not consult them, if a change in placement was proposed. In the USA, every child assessed as having special educational needs must, by law, have an Individual Education Plan, reviewed at least once a year with the full cooperation of the parents, who helped draw it up in the first place. These plans are a long way from the listing of arrangements for meeting special needs that the English system would include in a child's records. They are detailed; they describe goals in terms which are behavioural and so measurable; they are both a tool for ensuring that the children are getting the educational programme they need and a device for monitoring the success of the individual placement.

The American legislation has been operating only since 1977/8 and certainly by the end of the decade the hiccoughs were apparent. Although by the start of 1980 it was estimated that some four million children with disabilities were getting a better deal from the public school system than they had been earlier, it was not the older children or those whose disabilities were most severe who were benefiting most. Although it had been estimated that some 20,000 of the 85,000 additional special education teachers who would be needed to work the system would be at work within a few years, there was evidence that drawing up and working to Individual Education Plans was not easy. There was some evidence too that by no means all parents were in favour of mainstreaming, and that the dividing line between that and dumping had to be constantly reasserted. There was disquiet among some observers about the heavy bureaucracy that the Act had brought along with its safeguards of individual interest. And in 1980, the Education Advocates Coalition was able to indict the Federal Bureau for Education of the Handicapped for generally inadequate management of the system, pointing to still 'routine' exclusions from school, or placement in segregated settings, long waits for assessment and thousands of children left in institutions with little or no education at all.

That indictment could be echoed, however, outside the United States. And what that country had is what Britain, by the start of the 1980s, lacked: a framework of principle within which to make ordinary education special enough to meet the different needs of children who have disabilities. Over a hundred years ago, Samuel Gridley Howe, an American educator of more than ordinary perception, knew why that is important to them. 'Any class of young persons marked by an infirmity', he said,

depend more than ordinary persons do for their happiness and for their support, upon ties of kindred, of friendship and of neighbourhood. All these, therefore, ought to be nourished and strengthened during childhood and youth —

for it is then, and then only, that they take such deep root as to become strong and life lasting . . . Beware how you needlessly sever any of these ties . . . lest you make a homeless man, a wanderer and a stranger.[3]

And if making ordinary schools special enough to meet the needs of children who have disabilities is important to them, it is important too to the other children who use those schools as the basis of their own learning and exploration. It will offer them a chance to learn a lesson that is often now denied them: that the world in which they live is made up of people with a variety of abilities and inabilities and that that variety is a large one. It will offer them a perspective in which to live with the quota of abilities and inabilities that is their own — a perspective that is based on tolerance of difference, rather than its rejection. And in the arrangements that are made to meet the individual needs of children who have been defined as 'special', they could find the space to explore those of their own needs that are special too. Then schools could be on the way to becoming real places of learning and growth — for all children.

11

Work

The ex-docker doesn't know what is going to happen to him
and his family. He managed to get a job after his accident, but
as the doctor has told him and he knows well enough, it's not
the sort he needs. 'It's all that climbing and lifting. In wet
weather my leg plays up so that I've got to stay at home. Even
if I went, I'd never manage the wet pavements. They won't put
up with this for long. No firm would. I've been [to look for
work] today. But they say there's nothing for me.'

The widow in her early fifties has never found the effects
of the polio she had had as a child much of a hindrance
to her. 'I've always worked, and I've been in this factory
packing hairnets now for years. But it's no good. I can't
lift boxes like I used to. And they don't like it. I've been
worried stiff just lately. I know I shall have to leave.'

A man who had been off work after a serious accident
wondered how he'd manage when he got back to his old job.

After all, I looked quite normal when my workmates saw
me last. Now I can't move without sticks, callipers and a
steel corset. And I hadn't got on very well with the boss
before. No one was used to seeing really handicapped people
around the place; the most they had taken were people
with one eye or one finger off, or something. Well, when I
got there, they all stood around in a circle looking at me,
and no one seemed to know what to do. Then the boss
came along, and all he said was: 'Hello, it's nice to see you
back.' That was just right. If he had asked me how I was or
anything, I would have felt awful. As he was going out of
the door, I slipped on a patch of oil and down I went. No

one knew whether to help me up or what. I felt daft. The boss came back and said: 'And you can get up from there. I don't pay you for lying down all day.' That was fine — everything was back to normal.'[1]

People who work with their hands and muscles know what it would mean to them if their strength started to give out. The back ailments that are one of the commonest causes of days off work in Britain may be an irritation or an agony to the people who live with them; if those people are, say, dustmen, they can also spell the end of a job. Very many industrial workers know that industry has them in a fix, that the price of their jobs may be an eventual inability to go on doing them — or any job at all. Construction workers know the hazards of their trade to their physical abilities. Miners know what the toll of their trade can be on their limbs and lungs. Shipworkers know about deafness and chemical and other workers about the possibilities of poisoning. In the cities, the factories belch out the fumes that cause the bronchitis that seriously limits so many lives; in the country, agricultural machinery can bring its own quota of accidents. People who have less physically active jobs know that they don't escape, either. The London bus driver who takes less exercise than his colleague who collects the passengers' money is more at risk of coronary heart disease. The executive who eats, sits and worries too much knows what 'stress' means and he knows the risk of heart disease as well.

The way we work, in short, can be disabling. The number of industrial accidents may have dropped dramatically in the decade since the mid-1960s — in Britain, they fell from 757,000 to 478,000. The number of people who get one of the fifty-one recognized industrial diseases may have fallen too — from 20,000 to 12,000 in the first part of the 1970s. But we still know that the way we work can lead to disability and we put up with it, because often the alternative to a job that may disable may be no job at all.

There's no shortage of theorists to tell us what long-term unemployment can mean by way of handicap, to docket individual experience of its effects into the cycle of euphoria, loss of self-confidence, depression, and the final settling for a 'survival routine'. It may bring more than that. On the thesis of Dr Harvey Brenner of Johns Hopkins University, a one per cent rise in unemployment in the USA, sustained over six years, would yield 37,000 deaths, including 20,000 from cardiovascular disease, 1000 suicides, 600 homicides and 4,000 admissions to mental hospitals. If employment can exact disability as its price, the lack of it can not only disable but kill.

For a psychologist, who combined his own investigation of redundancy with four years of personal unemployment during the last nine, the experience is 'a nightmare', similiar in its effects to those reported for life imprisonment. 'I lost all sense of time and only the presence of my wife and family reminded me that weekends or holidays had arrived. I stopped worrying, for tomorrow was always the same as today. I had no hope, no future and was very depressed.'[2] The 'master and provider', as he found, may find himself dependent, taking over the household tasks while his wife goes out to work; while the role reversal may be just enough, it serves to emphasize the reversal of the working man's fortunes, his loss of contact with his accustomed world.

It is not, as it happens, disability that kept this man out of the job market, but the fact that social scientists were two a penny and often younger than he. But people of either sex who do have disabilities will find their own echoes in his experience. A woman of twenty-six, battling with severe loss of movement in her legs, put in for a retraining programme, and was rejected as unsuitable: 'I feel as if I have been put on the human rubbish tip.' A man of forty-seven was forced to retire because of heart and circulatory trouble; his wife finds the worst aspect of his disability not the restrictions that it imposes on their lives, but the 'devastating' psychological effect that it has had on him. She goes out to work and earns for the family; he stays home, does the chores and a little voluntary work, and feels useless. A middle-aged engineer who had to give up his job because of Parkinson's disease, knows the feeling only too well. He reckons himself lucky that his wife has a good job.

But it shouldn't be. It's against nature. It's the worst thing I've got to live with. A man should provide for his family. I did until four years ago. But now I've got to depend on my wife. It isn't right. I sit here thinking about it when she's out during the day, asking 'Why should it happen to me?' But there you are. What can you do about it?[3]

The unemployed man, goes on the phychologist, 'may at first feel optimistic, and think that he has the chance to start afresh. But applying for jobs, apart from being an expensive activity, leads to a pile of rejection letters. He is then told to be 'realistic' and devalues himself still further by applying for jobs way below his abilities and skills.'[4] A man who was the manager of a small plant, and lost his job not because of disability but because of business recession, knows what this can mean, after a year of unemployment and only ten interviews to show for the many more letters he has written: 'I feel embarrassed and a freak.' So does a man who used to be a top health administrator, who had to give up because of a progressive disease and is still applying for clerical posts. It is not just in today's economic climate that people know what it is to be pushed towards work that is below their capacities. A man with a successful career in social work is still glad that at one of the three interviews for a clerical job he culled from 180 applications, he met someone who told him to stop undervaluing himself just because he had severe disabilities. But if he hadn't met such a response, he wonders, where would he be, twenty years on?

He was fortunate. Many people, whatever the cause of their unemployment, will settle for a job that under-uses their skills rather than continue in it. So a quality examiner in a steel plant, made redundant not because of disability but because the plant closed, settled eventually for a job as a filing clerk, because at the age of forty-seven he left he couldn't afford to be choosy: 'There's little job satisfaction, but it's better than doing nothing.' So a man whose bronchitis forced him to give up his engineering job had very little choice: 'They sent me down to this factory and gave me a bucket and a mop and told me to get on with washing the floors. I've been doing that ever since.' But he might count himself relatively lucky, even so. By one British reckoning, a quarter of disabled people in professional work and nearly two-thirds of those in unskilled work have to give it up and leave the job market altogether.

While the experience of unemployment may be equally grim for individuals whether they have disabilities or not, very many more who do will know it. By 1978, when the general unemployment rate in Britain was six per cent, the rate among people on the Department of Employment's register of disabled workers was fourteen per cent. By the end of the decade, nearly sixty per cent of the 485,000 people on that register had been out of work for longer than a year, compared with about a quarter of unemployed workers in the country as a whole. Nor is this the whole story, as very many people with disabilities are not on that register. The incidence of unemployment among people with spinal injuries, with mental retardation, who have had a mental illness, may be nearer one-third.

By 1980, when total unemployment in Britain was at its highest since the 1930s, the relative position of people with disabilities was likely to be getting worse yet. Employers could afford to be choosy. Older workers who had become redundant, who found themselves in competition with those who were younger, more confident and cheaper to hire, knew what this meant. So, if a 1980 survey of employers' attitudes to people who are overweight is anything to go by, did they. But if any group will know what discrimination means, it is likely to be the one made up of people with disabilities. The man who got two interviews from fifty applications when he presented his considerable qualifications together with information about his restricted mobility, and thirteen interviews from thirty-five applications when he kept quiet about this, will not be the only one who has met discrimination in action. And if many workers now settle for jobs which are below their capacity, that is true for not just some people with disabilities, but around half of them. The blind woman who started her career in the Civil Service as a typist, took seven years to become a secretary, longer yet to get higher promotion and reckons to have been underemployed for far too long, will know how that can feel over the years.

So, by 1980, one Western society at least, based firmly on the notion that it is 'normal' for men, and increasingly women, to work through the majority of their adult years, was telling more and more of them that they were excluded from this 'normal' expectation. That raises questions for us all. Some of them go way beyond the scope of this book. Others are more immediately relevant, and they are relevant whether our country happens to be in economic recession or not. Are we to draw the boundaries of 'normal' ability that make up an 'acceptable worker' more and more tightly? Or are we going to try to widen those boundaries to ensure that no group of workers is more unemployed than any other?

There is nothing at all in disability as such that says that the people who live with it 'can't work'. The American President's Committee on Employment of the Handicapped knows that well enough, and in its energetic propaganda is working to make sure that employers know it too. There is research enough to back it — especially now that the Vietnam war has added its impetus. If people with disabilities do get the chance to work, as pretty well every study of their performance shows, they are more reliable and meticulous than others — perhaps because they know they have to be. Britain has been slow to make parallel studies. But at the end of the 1960s, the eleven per cent of the British workforce who had one or more disablement conditions — and over 400,000 of them with appreciable or severe incapacity — was bearing out research findings by simply getting on with the job. So while no one could claim that each and every person with a disability could and should work, it is clear enough, and has been for years, that very many of them have been denied that opportunity. Their disability, with which they must live, has been overlaid by some powerful and damaging handicaps, which are not inevitable at all.

They may find themselves handicapped by employers' own lack of understanding; research which appears mostly in professional medical or rehabilitation publications is hardly well placed to dispel the handicaps of prejudice and ignorance with which many employers are living. They may find themselves handicapped either in finding work at all, or in their choice of jobs, by many of the factors we have already looked at. The handicaps imposed by unadapted public transport don't just limit social opportunities; they limit working ones as well. The handicaps imposed by inaccessible buildings don't just restrict choice in spending a day out; they limit working lives. The 'safety' regulations that restrict people's access to cinemas may, in a different form, keep them out of workplaces. People may be handicapped by their own lack of marketable skills; the disability that comes during a working life hits hardest at the manual workers who are precisely the people whose expertise, once lost, leaves them with little else to offer. But as well as any or all of this, people with disabilities may find themselves handicapped by the very systems set up to prepare them for, and find them a place in, the job market.

We have seen something of the effects that the low expectations of special schools can have on the prospects of their students. A study by the British National Children's Bureau in the mid-1970s shows just what this can mean for a cross-section of eighteen-year-olds with learning difficulties and other disabilities, who are trying to find their way in the adult world. They might be thought, for a start, to be first candidates for the further education that could boost their skills to the maximum. But only five per cent of them were still at school, or in further education, compared to nearly a third of their 'able' contemporaries. Entering the workforce, they found themselves already set up for disadvantage; although three-fifths of those in work were in industrial-manual jobs, they were less likely than their contemporaries to have apprenticeships. They were also less likely to have found the sort of work they wanted, even though their aspirations were very low. They were more likely to be doing work which involved heavy lifting all or nearly all the time, and more likely to be working long hours. They were four times as unlikely to have facilities at work like indoor lavatories, a canteen and opportunities to make tea and coffee. They were three times as likely to feel insecure and four times as likely to feel unhappy. And already they were more than twice as likely to have had some spells of unemployment than their contemporaries who were also in the job market.

So young people with disabilities are caught again in the

cycle of low expectation. Low aspirations for them at school put little pressure on the further education establishments which could help them gain more skills to offer on a hostile labour market. There is evidence enough that adult education colleges, for instance, have been slow to offer courses that enable young people with learning difficulties to continue their education, or to adapt their premises and their teaching to meet the needs of others with physical or sensory disabilities. If it weren't for the Open University, whose students are based at home and work mainly through correspondence and radio and television, and which is very conscious of the need to adapt its methods to the special needs of students with different physical and sensory disabilities, the prospects in British higher education would be very slim for those whose disabilities are severe. The Warnock Committee on special educational needs put the development of further education opportunities as one of its top priorities, and although the subsequent economic climate made rapid improvement unlikely, at least an awareness was beginning to grow. But even if awareness was translated into action, increased skills will not mean much in market terms unless the system designed to help people get jobs is effective. At the moment, it can actually seem to hinder them.

Donald Jones started his working life as an apprentice paint-sprayer. He got on well with the job and with his fellow-workers. Over the years, he moved on and got different jobs without difficulty. But then he went to the Job Centre to find work. He was asked why he didn't drive; he explained that this was because he had epilepsy. The interviewer 'seemed to go a little beserk'. He asked why Donald Jones had never declared this, never registered as disabled. So then he did and he wishes he hadn't. He deliberately avoided then, as he had before, applying for any job that involved heavy machinery or could bring any hazard to himself or others; he reckons that he has always known his own capacities well. But now that he was registered as disabled, his prospects seemed to have changed.

He recounts his experiences with one prospective employer:

He made me feel the lowest of the low, with comments like; 'What made you think you would get a job here? Our workforce wouldn't stand you working with them.' The form was ripped up and thrown in the bin in less than a quarter of an hour. One person had set me back years. I walked out of there in a daze. I didn't, I couldn't, look back. I started to walk, then run, I ran the one-and-a-half miles back to where I lived. Once inside, I just broke down and cried in my girl-friend's arms.

He is now in sheltered employment and feels some bitterness. 'Given the chance, disabled people are just as good as, if not better in their jobs, than "normal" people. But there is no chance, never will be, in spite of all those well-intentioned people who try to help our cause. Society as a whole will never change their attitudes towards disability.'

We have seen something of the cycle of expectation which the Disablement Resettlement Officers, who in Britain are charged with finding work for people with disabilities, may perpetuate. Although some people speak highly of their efforts, others find that they, and the whole special employment system of which they are part, can make finding work not easier but harder. Leave aside the attitudes, what about the behaviour that that system encourages?

Under it, every firm with more than twenty employees is supposed to reserve three per cent of its jobs for workers with disabilities. But the law is widely disregarded; by the end of the 1970s, only about a third of firms complied with it. They have only ever been ten prosecutions for breaking the law, and the fines for doing so have not gone up since the system was introduced after the war. The administrators of the system sign the papers that excuse firms from compliance as a matter of routine. The public sector, which might be thought to be in a position to give a lead, does not. Central government departments accept a moral, though not a legal obligation, but give no lead either. By 1979, only one department met its quota and that was neither the Department of Employment, nor the Department of Health, where the Minister for the Disabled has his offices. People with disabilities had by then increasingly given up on the scheme; even if all those who had chosen to register under it were found jobs, the national quota compliance rate would rise from 1.7 per cent to only 2.1 per cent.

The Government used this failure of the system to suggest twice during the 1970s that the whole notion of quota should be abolished. It was putting its money instead on persuasion – and certainly some 50,000 people with disabilities, both on and off the register, were found jobs in one year. But if the law has been unsuccessful, will the persuasive guidelines of the official Fit to Work Scheme do any better?

The United States has found that persuasion is not enough. Although it has no quota scheme, it uses the law in a different way. Under the 1973 Rehabilitation Act, the Federal Government is obliged to take the lead in the hiring and promotion of people with disabilities. Contracts between the Government and individual firms must contain a clause declaring non-discrimination, unless 'undue business hardship' would result from hiring people in this category. Firms must also submit an 'affirmative action' plan which includes the removal of architectural barriers, launching of recruitment campaigns, modification of job specifications, arrangements for training workers with disabilities and the provision of 'reasonable accommodation in offices and factories'. The components of these plans are not very different from the guidelines of the British Fit for Work campaign. The difference is that while British employers who follow these guidelines may get a desk ornament and a wall plaque to prove it, American employers who don't produce their plans stand to lose their Federal contracts and possibly end up in court as well.

The drawback to the system is that it applies only to the Government and firms which do business with it. There is a carrot to entice them into line in the shape of tax credits for employing people with disabilities – but only as one of seven specified disadvantaged groups. It is West Germany which seems to have come nearest to cracking the problem, with a system that writes in the stick in a way that employers can't avoid and provides the carrot as well.

There is a quota and it is high – six per cent of the workforce for any firm employing more than sixteen people. For every place that should go to a worker with a disability but doesn't, the firm must pay a levy into a central fund which is used to create employment opportunities for these people. For every worker employed above the quota, firms draw a subsidy from the fund; they can also draw on it for training programmes and employment aids for workers with disabilities. There is no shortage of them on the register — presumably because, unlike the British one, it is seen to work. National compliance with the quota was, at the end of the 1970s, running at about five per cent and workers whose disabilities were severe were not being excluded.

Some people find special subsidies to employers distasteful, in that they reinforce the damaging and inaccurate notion of workers who have a disability as being also workers who are a 'burden'. But in a world with little time for philosophical niceties, the overwhelming advantage of the West German scheme is that it seems to work. It does not depend on vigorous enforcement, either by civil servants or by the courts. It ensures that the section of the community which is called 'employer' fulfils its obligations indirectly, through payments to the central fund, even if it is not willing to do so directly. A model like this seems to offer the best hope of ensuring what is, after all, not a very ambitious return: that workers with disabilities end up not twice as unemployed as the rest of the workforce or more, but simply unemployed in the same proportion.

The model means not just more opportunities for workers with disabilities to join a working place which has been adapted to strip away the handicaps of access and advancement which so often now stand between them and it. It means too a more general expansion of opportunity than this.

The central fund could be used, as it is in West Germany, to expand sheltered work. People who are mentally retarded, in Britain as elsewhere, have a particularly crying need for this sort of opportunity. What they are offered now can be a very literal 'make-work' in those special 'training centres' set up for them: there is not much that affirms your sense of worth to your community in hooking rugs for the staff to unhook so that tomorrow there are rugs to hook.

The fund could be used to provide launching capital and seed money for cooperatives or small businesses set up by, or employing a large proportion of, workers who are registered as disabled. There is no shortage of aspiration. There may even be, as in the American Office of Minority Business Enterprise, the technical and managerial assistance for people who want to make a start. But there may be a serious shortage of funds. If people with severe mental retardation can, after the training they need and a thorough analysis of the tasks to be fulfilled, participate in the production of whatever it is that the American National Aeronautical and Space Administration needs to go about its business, then others elsewhere can make their own start in their own way.

The fund could be used to hire production lines in factories so that workers with disabilities get opportunities for more realistic on-the-job training than they are offered now. The Eastern Nebraska Community Office of Retardation has been using this method of introducing its customers to the rewards as well as the demands of the working world for some years now. The fund could be used to pay individual, established workers to guide individuals who are mentally retarded – and maybe other young workers as well – through the initial intricacies of mastering the social and technical skills that a job may demand; the National Society for Mentally Handicapped Children and Adults has pioneered such a system in England with great success. And these schemes are perhaps only the beginning of opportunity for workers with different disabilities. The essential starting-point is the recognition that they have the right to be as employed or unemployed as anyone else; neither more nor less.

There is a fashion in the current economic situation of some of our Western societies to look at things rather differently. People with disabilities, so it's said, are in a unique position to teach us all about the age that is coming on us, the age where leisure is the forty-hour a week business, and what we used to know as work will fill the cracks between business hours, for more and more sections of the population. The people who put about such theories are usually employed, and with tenure, in university departments. They could do worse, perhaps, than to listen to the views of those they would cast

162

as pioneers, who know that they are living now and not in some hypothetical future.

A group of young people who are mentally retarded, to take just one example, is discussing why work is important. For them there is no question: 'It's what you do, isn't it?' Work is the passport to the adult world: you work 'because Dad does'. Work is the accepted way of making your contribution to your society: 'If I didn't go to work, people wouldn't get their evening papers.' Work brings its own satisfaction: 'I really enjoy seeing the floor all clean, I like it when the room smells nice.'[5]

Individuals who have disabilities may choose the pioneering way. Others may, in any realistic terms, have it forced on them; what that can mean we look at next. But what we need to remember first is that very many people with disabilities want to work, and that they are unnecessarily handicapped in that very ordinary aspiration. And we might remember too that workplaces which are adapted to their needs, and flexible enough to encompass them, are workplaces which are likely to be less handicapping, more human and more attuned to the needs of all their workers — whether those workers have a disability or whether they don't.

12

Economics

The teacher who had to give up her job because of a progressive disability would probably count her family fairly financially secure. But, as she knows: 'Disability is an expensive occupation. You cannot shop around, you need more heat, travel is expensive, so is extra equipment. When I was able-bodied, I used to cure the blues by buying something new — if only a pair of knickers! Now at least I can save that money, because shopping is a major undertaking.'

When the husband of the woman with severe multiple sclerosis left home, he took their financial security with him, and she is now bringing up their two sons. Their fares to school and clothes are expensive. They live on a hilltop, so she relies on the corner store for food, and that is expensive too. Her social worker doesn't seem to know the ins and outs of benefit entitlements any better than she does; what she does know is that she has been waiting a long time for her claim to be settled. Meanwhile, what used to seem necessities have become luxuries.

The father who receives invalidity benefit thinks he's getting near the end of his tether. His son, with whom he lives, is now eighteen and has profound mental retardation. He isn't clear about benefit entitlement for the young man, so he now receives less than he might do. They get a little money towards laundry costs, but it only covers a quarter of the bill. What's really worrying the father is that his own benefit has been withdrawn, and he doesn't understand why. Surely it can't be because he's been working for those few hours to try to boost their income?

The divorced woman with arthritis finds that she can make do — just. She goes to bed early to save heating costs and she has cut fruit out of her diet as a dispensible luxury. What really hurt, she says, is when the colleagues with whom she does voluntary work decided to go out to lunch and she knew she couldn't afford to join them.

The young man with cerebral palsy also knows what social restriction can mean. He has no problems in basic living, because he's in a publicly-run residential home. But that means, too, that he gets only 'pocket money' benefit, and that doesn't leave much room for exploration. Because he can, with difficulty, walk four hundred yards, he doesn't qualify for the special benefit paid to people who are unable, or virtually unable, to walk. But there is more than four hundred yards between his home and the shops, cinema and library; he must take a taxi to get to them, and that is expensive. He can reach the pub on foot, and that he enjoys. But he sits alone, because he daren't be put in the position of looking too mean to stand a round of drinks.

There is the story of the people with leprosy who lived in a separated, far-off village. They got little help; they were poor even by the standard of their country. But the visitor noticed among them a certain solidarity, a spirit of cooperation. Then the village got some of the help it so urgently needed. When the visitor returned a couple of years later, he was impressed by the efficiency and industry with which the village had built on this. But he noticed that some of the villagers whose disabilities had been most severe were no longer around; he asked after them. Oh well, he was told, they couldn't work, so we sent them away.

The complex packages of goods, services and cash benefits which have grown up for people with disabilities in Western societies can often trace their beginnings to rehabilitation schemes launched with the declared aim of getting back to work people disabled in successive wars. We have seen clearly enough in the last chapter how much more still needs to be done if people with disabilities are to have equal opportunities on the job market. But necessary though this is, it raises its own questions. It raises questions about the quality of work, and the relative economic position of those who do manage to get jobs. It raises quite distinct and quite central questions about what happens to all those people who, because of severity of disability or age, are out of the job market altogether. It raises questions about economic need and its recognition. Our societies being what they are, those questions in turn raise others about the hierarchy of worth into which those societies slot their members. And those are questions for us all.

A central fact of the lives of very many people with disabilities is a simple one: they are poor. Many others will know the handicaps that this brings to individual lives. But people with disabilities, as a group, are more likely to know them than most. And, if their disabilities are severe, they will have less room for manoeuvre, because they will have to spend more of their income simply on keeping going.

In his monumental survey, *Poverty in the United Kingdom,* Peter Townsend concluded that more than half the people with appreciable or severe incapacity were, a decade ago, in households which were either poor, or on the margins of poverty, by the State's own subsistence standard — and that compared to one-fifth of the 'ordinary' population. This was not just because disability increases with age, and elderly people can expect to be poorer than those at work. In each major age group, people with disabilities were poorer than people without them. It was not, either, just because more people with disabilities are unable to work. Even those in the workforce were poorer than other workers. They must very often, as we have seen, settle for jobs which do not use their skills; they may have fewer skills to offer in the first place; they may be limited by their disability in the hours they can work. Whatever the reason, they will end up disproportionately in jobs which are badly paid. When Townsend made his survey, about a third of working men were earning below 80% of the mean. But even for men whose disabilities were slight, that proportion rose to 45%. And it rose, too, with age. Nearly a quarter of men in their fifties with more severe incapacities were earning below 60% of the mean, compared with only 12% of their contemporaries who had no disability. And while 12% of the second group also had earnings of more than 140% of the man, only 7% of the first could claim the same.

And yet while disability brings disproportionately low

income, it also brings disproportionately high costs. The connection starts early. Children with a physical disability or disturbed behaviour can wear clothes out faster than others. They may need special toys or books to stimulate them, as may children who are deaf. There may be extra costs in travelling to clinics and other places which help them develop. And family resources to meet these costs can be low. In one British study, only a quarter of the mothers felt able to go out to work, compared to about half the married women in the population as a whole; over three-quarters of the fathers felt restricted, because of their child's disability, in their job mobility or their ability to take on overtime.

For adults with disabilities, the costs can mount. Those who work, even if their job is a good one, may find themselves caught in a cycle: they have to keep working to earn the money that enables them to go to work. As one woman points out, she needs an electric wheelchair for her job, and it costs a lot to keep it working; if her car is out of commission, she has to take expensive taxis; she has to look presentable for her public, and that means meeting the high costs of wear and tear on her clothes. The expenditure is more than worth it to her. But for very many people with disabilities, a well-paid job, or any job at all, is out of reach. Yet the costs of their disability must be met.

They may find it hard, if not impossible, to shop around — so it's the nearest shop, whether it is the most expensive or not. They may have to pay others to do the sort of household jobs that most people do for themselves, like painting, decorating or gardening. They may have to buy their own essential aids and equipment — certainly in the United States, and often even in Britain, where public provision is far more developed. The standard National Health Service hearing aid, for instance, doesn't work for people with the most severe hearing loss, so they must buy their own. They must also, if they are deaf, find the money for basic tools for ordinary living like a vibrator alarm clock, flashing doorbell and adaptation to their telephone. The battery-powered wheelchairs which are essential to the independent mobility of people with very severe physical disabilities must usually be bought privately. One widow of seventy-two has spent all her savings on keeping hers on the road, and half the money she had set aside for her burial as well; she can now no longer afford to run the thing, and is reliant on State benefits, which she and her husband swore she would never be. Local authorities, as we have seen, are empowered to make adaptations to housing, but people must usually make their own contribution to any that are extensive.

With basic costs like this, simply to sustain a life which is as 'normal' as possible, people with disabilities will find that their opportunities for even ordinary social pleasures can be very limited. Even if they can afford them, the price, to them, will again often be high. As one woman who is chair-bound points out, the only place in the theatre that can accommodate her is the most expensive one, the only hotels which can welcome her are the grandest. More often, what is part of the normal expectation of enjoyment for many others will become luxury for people with disabilities.

So Townsend found that nearly three-quarters of the people whose incapacities were appreciable or severe had not had a week's holiday away from home that year, compared to half the rest of the population; while this may have been partly to do with the difficulties of travel and accommodation, it also had substantially to do with cash. He assessed the numbers of people who had missed at least one cooked meal in the past two weeks, or had not invited a relative to a meal or snack in the past month, or did not have common household goods like television, radio, or telephone. The pleasures were simple enough – and yet people with disabilities, already often at risk of isolation, were more deprived of them than the rest of the population. Aids to living, like refrigerators or washing machines, are commonplace enough, too – yet people with disabilities, already bound to find the sheer 'dailiness' of life harder than most, were more deprived of them as well. And their degree of deprivation went up, not down, with the severity of their disability.

Since Townsend made his study, different countries have been building on their own efforts to mitigate the poverty which is so central a fact of life for so many people with disabilities, and some are doing it more successfully than others.

168

The bewildering systems of benefits in cash and kind are bringing help to very many people. But there are three common drawbacks to these schemes.

The first, in Britain at least, is that in spite of a proliferation of benefits, the relative position of people with disabilities as a group has not appreciably changed. By the end of the 1970s, the Royal Commission on the Distribution of Income and Wealth concluded that more than half the families whose head was 'permanently disabled' — and so by definition out of the job market — were living at below 120% of the poverty line, and that those whose disabilities were most severe also headed the poorest families. When it reported, 38% of single men with disabilities, and 31% of married men, two-thirds of single women and 12% of married ones in the same category were living at the poverty line or below it.

The second drawback to the proliferating schemes of help in cash and kind is that they have their own built-in rationing devices: they are so complex that people often simply don't know how to claim their due. The fault is a common one, whether in the United States, where local, State and Federal provision jostle together, or in Britain, where a whole 'welfare rights' industry has grown up over the past decade, whose first rationale is purely and simply to help people through the benefit maze. Should that job be necessary? At least one man with a severe disability thinks not. The most wearisome part of his condition is simply 'having to fight for everything — even what you know you are entitled to'.

The third drawback to the schemes is more fundamental, and would exist even if all the people got all of their due all of the time. While the bewildering system of benefits may be beginning to redress the gross inequity of resources between people who have disabilities and those who do not, the price of this achievement may be greater, not less, inequity among people with disabilities themselves. So it is not only possible, but often entirely likely, that two people whose degree of disability is exactly similar are treated in two completely different ways. The result will be that, in very real terms, one will be 'worth' more than the other. The flaw is as unjust as it is fundamental. But it is proving extremely hard to heal, because its roots are deep in the values – little discussed, but none the less real – that our societies put on people with disabilities. Social security and welfare schemes express four common value judgements. Not all schemes share all of them, and their strength will vary from country to country and from time to time within each country. But they crop up often enough to bear examination.

The first value judgement has to do with the relative 'worth' of people who have 'contributed' to their society and those who have not. From the USSR to the USA to Britain and beyond, people who acquired their disability in service to their country in time of war get the most generous treatment of all those who have disabilities. It may, as in the USSR, include the right to go to the head of various food and commodity queues; in most countries, it will include a higher pension than that awarded to others with disabilities which may be exactly similar. In Britain at least, that pension is not based on degree of disability within even this restricted group, but on the rank the pensioner held at time of active service.

Reward for 'contribution' is also expressed in the level of pensions to those disabled in their service to industry. Industrial pensions in European countries are characteristically higher than those awarded to people who may have similiar disabilities, and may also be forced out of the job market during their working years, but who cannot pin the cause to industrial accident or disease. And finally, the 'contribution' that people make through their working lives may be very directly recognized in the level of their pensions. In Britain, those who have made their payments to the National Insurance Scheme while in work get higher pensions – whether in old age or if disability forces them out of the job market – than those who have not been able to 'contribute' in this way.

This hierarchy of worth has been dented in recent years. People who have never, because of a severe disability from childhood, been part of the workforce, may now get a specific benefit as of right, rather than having to rely on the subsistence level financial aid available to 'non-contributors'. But, in Britain at least, that pension is still pitched so low that the subsistence aid may be worth more to them. There are other anomalies:

170

married women who have a severe disability and have not been 'contributors' had, in 1980, to prove not only their incapacity for work but their inability to perform 'normal household duties' before they qualified for the pension at all. And the notion of the value of the 'contributor' is still being reinforced. Although the extra costs of childhood disability still brought no specific allowance by 1980, British parents who could prove that their child's disability had been caused by one of the vaccines urged in public health programmes could claim a special payment; these children had, after all, made their 'contribution' to society by upholding its general well-being.

The approach is ingrained; the very system of pensions may depend on it. So the value judgement it sustains may seem nothing but 'normal', even proper. But is it? Is an individual's contribution limited to the measurable sort on which the system depends?

The second value judgement which systems of social security and welfare reflect is allied to the first. It has to do with 'rewarding the able' — concentrating resources on those who, though not 'contributors' now, may well become so in future. This is at the back of most rehabilitation provision and has been one of the mainsprings of much recent activity on behalf of American citizens with disabilities, given its impetus by the aftermath of another war. Turning people into 'tax-payers not tax-takers' has proved a powerful slogan for the enlistment of public support and — as the major fund-raisers for people with mental retardation in Canada were finding by the mid-seventies — not just in the United States, either.

If 'rewarding the able' finds its expression most clearly in rehabilitation and fund-raising programmes, it has its echoes elsewhere too. They are there in the tax concessions that both the USA and Britain make to people who are blind — which is useful to those who are tax-payers but of no use at all to the large majority, who are not. They are there in the concessionary passes for public transport issued to people who are elderly or have disabilities — which are of benefit to those who are 'able' enough to use public transport, but of none whatever to those whose disabilities are most severe. They are there in the British arrangement for people to put their Mobility Allowance towards the cost of a car — which is helpful to people who are 'able' to find other income to cover conversion and running costs, but of no use at all to people who cannot.

'Rewarding the able' may make some sense in sheer cost-benefit terms; if for a small investment, after all, people can gain large benefits, surely the investment is worth making; and one day, perhaps, we will, their independence assured, have money left over for those who, because of the severity of their disability, offer less return. The trouble with this line of reasoning is that that day doesn't come. The obverse of 'rewarding the able' is penalizing those who are not. Wholehearted concentration on rehabilitation for work leaves out those for whom rehabilitation may be, simply, for living more fully. Tax concessions to one small group are likely to mean less attention to the financial needs of those who do not pay taxes because they are too poor. Passes for ordinary public transport are likely to mean less thought for the kind that people whose disabilities are more severe can use. Rewarding the able can mean that those who need the most help get the least. It leads, at the limit, to those 'special care' wards in British mental retardation institutions, and the back wards of similar places all over the West.

There have been efforts over recent years to redress the balance, to assert a value judgement that says people whose disabilities are severe also have the right to the help they may need, and not in expectation of return, either. Not the least important aspect of the promised Federal funding for the Alternative Living Movement programmes that we met in 'The Cycle of Expectation' is the official recognition that people have the right to help to live decently, not simply to work. The British allowances paid to people whose mobility is most severely restricted, or who need a great deal of personal attention by night or day, express the same value.

The humanitarian impulse can't be doubted; neither can the benefit that the British allowances have brought to a large number of people. But the trouble with benefits payable to only a small and restricted section of the population is that people must go through hoops to get them. The young man with cerebral palsy whom we met at the start of this chapter didn't get through the hoop that led to Mobility Allowance at all; we have seen the restrictions that this has meant to him. The man with one leg who walks, with difficulty, on crutches, didn't get through the hoop, either. So he decided to appeal. To do that, he had to go to an office set up for the purpose. And to reach the office, he had to take himself and his crutches, slowly, with difficulty, up no fewer than twenty-eight stairs. And when he got to the top, he eventually lost his appeal, because he had, slowly and with difficulty, made his way up twenty-eight stairs to lodge it. The trouble with specific and restricted benefits, as at present administered, is that there is always someone unjustly left on the wrong side of them. The trouble with these benefits, as we saw in the comments on married women's benefit in 'The Cycle of Expectation', and as the man on crutches confirms, is that people may have to underplay their abilities to get through the hoop at all.

This side-effect of trying to channel help where it is most needed becomes a value in itself. People are seen as 'worth' helping just *because* they are 'helpless' and so 'deserving'. And keeping them that way seems to become part of the plan. The tendency is seen most clearly in the disincentives to work which are built into both the American and the British benefit systems. Although by 1980 there were plans in the United States to overhaul the arrangements, it remained true that people with severe disabilities who nevertheless wanted to work stood to lose not just benefits but entitlement to Medicare — which, given the low earnings of many people with disabilities, was a powerful disincentive. In something of the same way, people in Britain who want to work part-time despite severe disability may find that their benefit is cut, to leave them worse off in work than they would be out of it. Only war and industrial pensioners, who can earn as much as they like on top of their benefit, are free from this disincentive.

The tendency to keep people financially dependent is built in, too, in all those services which substitute kind for cash. It is at its strongest in those institutions which offer 'training' or 'care'. So in their special day centres in many Western countries, people who are mentally retarded work hard on industrial contracts which other workers only tolerate because of the financial return for their boredom. But people who are mentally retarded get the boredom without the financial return — because they are not 'workers', but are receiving a service. At worst this is sheer exploitation; at best, it is a poor training indeed for taking your place in a world whose transactions are mostly made in money. British sheltered workshops have echoes of this system; there, the 'service' is paid for by their workers in wages which are well below the equivalent in open industry. As one man says, 'Whilst we can be proud that we support ourselves, if a "normal" person was asked to do the work which we do and take the wages that we do, they would laugh and tell them to get lost.'

Residential institutions have their own echoes of the tendency. Because in Britain they are a publicly-funded service, their inhabitants get, as their only guaranteed income, the 'pocket money' rate of the basic pension — and the amount is as sure to perpetuate financial dependence as the name is to perpetuate the perception of recipients as childish and irresponsible. And the dependence is perpetuated too in all those payments in kind rather than cash which have been made in Britain in recent years, whether these are telephones, holidays or aids. Very many people with disabilities see nothing wrong with these at all, and welcome them, just as they welcome the concessionary bus passes. They are probably wise to, as the money for which they are a substitute is not in sight. But it is worth pointing out that these payments in kind simply reinforce the perception of people with disabilities as helpless — unable to handle a decent income for themselves and to decide which aids, what holiday, whether five bus-rides or one taxi.

And perhaps, in the end, it suits our societies to ensure that people remain financially 'helpless', dependent on whatever benefit or service will be offered next. A decent income in place of the bewildering complexes of cash and kind, paid as of right, would be perhaps too much like a recognition of people with disabilities as full citizens, with choices to make and the means to make those choices effective.

In Britain, the plan for that income has existed ever since 1965, when the Disablement Income Group first started campaigning. A decade later, the battle was taken up by the Disability Alliance, which represents some sixty organizations of and for people with disabilities. In essence, both schemes encompass the same provision. First, a non-taxable allowance, designed to cover the myriad of extra costs which disability can bring, would be payable according not to the cause of disability but to its severity, and whether people are in work or out of it. The second element in the scheme would have to do with income maintenance: it would be payable in full to people who could not work at all and on a sliding scale to those whose earnings were restricted because of disability, at a rate which abolished the current discrimination against 'non-contributors'. The scheme would bring equity of treatment to everyone with a disability, irrespective of its cause or their status. It would, for the first time, recognize the extra costs of disablement. It would remove the present disincentives to work, so bringing Britain into line with other countries in the European Economic Community. It would, finally, go some way towards tackling the poverty in which so many people with disabilities are now forced to live.

Successive Governments have pledged support for the outlines of the scheme. Successive Governments have said that the country cannot afford it. But in 1979 there was a Government plan to introduce a standard concession on the nation's buses for people who were elderly or disabled. It had its merits. It would bring equality of treatment across the land. It would certainly do the nation's bus companies no harm to have their business boosted out of rush-hours. It would cost only fifty million pounds, and the money seemed to be there.

The scheme was also, of course, a classic example of 'rewarding the able', failing to bring help to the people whose deprivation was greatest and reinforcing the notion that people with disabilities need hand-outs in kind rather than opportunities for individual choice. And for less than half the sum that the scheme would have cost, the Government could have guaranteed a decent income to people whose disabilities were most severe.

In the end, the scheme was dropped. We are left with the mixture of benefits in cash and kind and the system which, in

175

Britain as elsewhere, reflects some of society's deepest judgements about what people with disabilities are 'worth'. And we are left, too, with the questions that those judgements raise.

'Obviously we who are disabled', says Paul Hunt in 'A Criticial Condition',

are deeply affected by the assumptions of our uselessness which surround us. But it is vital that we should not accept this devaluation of ourselves, yearning only to be able to earn our livings and thus prove our worth. We do not have to prove anything. If we have a basic willingness to contribute to the community, yet cannot do an ordinary job, we may certainly contribute in less obvious ways . . . Our freedom from the competitive trappings that accompany work in our society may give us the opportunity to demonstrate its essential elements. Also we can act as a symbol for the pre-eminent claims of non-utilitarian values, a visible challenge to anyone who treats his job as a final end in itself . . . At the ultimate point, we may only be able to suffer, to be passive through complete physical inability . . . Those who lead active lives are perhaps especially inclined to ignore man's need to accept passivity in relation to so many forces beyond his control. They may need reminding sometimes of our finiteness, our feminine side in the hands of fate or providence. We are well placed to do this job at least.

13

Politics

'We wanted to do everything ourselves. That was the important thing — for us to get out and speak for ourselves, to let people know that we are here on this earth, that we're not just put away, locked behind doors or locked in boxes. We've got a voice. We can speak for ourselves. We all wanted our own personal lives.' So Valerie Schaaf, first president of People First, explained why a group of people who are mentally retarded decided to hold the first large conference in the United States, for others in the same category. People First has grown since, in the States and Canada too, part of the strengthening self-advocacy movement. It doesn't just hold conferences. Its members may help each other overcome the barriers that trip them up in daily living; they help professional workers and parents overcome their handicaps in understanding; they help the public that watches television and listens to the radio do the same; they help government officials understand the services that are going to lead to individual growth.

For many years, there were only organizations *for* the disabled, primarily composed of able-bodied people determining what they felt were the needs of disabled people. But recently, organizations *of* the disabled have been created, for several reasons. Disabled people felt that organizations for the disabled were not listening to disabled people and therefore not presenting their concerns adequately or at all. Disabled people also felt that they did not have a voice in planning and implementing programmes run by organizations *for* the disabled ... Disabled people were concerned that able-bodied people were speaking for them, and doing the jobs that they should do themselves. Disabled people wanted a piece of the action; they wanted to determine their own destinies; they wanted to do away with parental concern and sympathetic caretaking . . . And after hard work, and even harder-fought battles that are part of any creation, disabled people have achieved their goal. Disabled people are running the show, organizing meetings, being sought as *the* spokespeople in issues relevant to disability. Their leadership role has been recognized by the media, the government and even by the organizations *for* the disabled, who have relinquished their position to some degree.

So Diane Lattin, editor of *Disabled USA*, summed up a decade of progress in 1979.

Times are changing, and not just in North America, either. 'Full equality and participation' was the theme of the International Year of Disabled People in 1981. But the first thing its organizers did was to change the name to suit the theme. They had to. The first title, after all, had been the International Year *for* Disabled Persons. The change is not just semantic; it is a recognition of a growing shift in the politics of disability, and a radical one at that.

It is a shift that very many people would recognize. Equality of opportunity is the benchmark for people who happen to be black, or women, or are fighting from their own minority position. Measures against discrimination may be more or less formal, or not yet part of the social fabric at all. Debate continues, more or less fruitfully, on the sort of positive discrimination that may be needed to reach the point where equality of opportunity means anything at all. Participation in decisions that affect our lives is a call to replace our crumbling faith in our social institutions and those who run them, whether we are members of a tenants' or residents' association, seeking industrial democracy, more local rather than central government, or less government at all. Participation in the fruits of our work is at the back of the calls for profit-sharing in industry and the modification of academic examination systems. In the challenge of the new politics of disability, in its chequered progress, in its formulations and its set-backs, there is an echo for anyone involved in any of the new politics and anyone who rejects them as well.

There is a challenge, first, to traditional concepts of charitable endeavour for people who are, by definition, to be 'done to', who are seen as helpless, pitiable and best represented by fund-raisers who want to be successful, as children and cute at that. As the American car sticker says: 'You gave me your dimes, now give me a job'. There's a challenge to traditional charitable organizations, as the venerable British Royal National Institute *for* the Blind found out in the early 1970s, when the National Federation *of* the Blind launched its campaign for 'an equal say in our own affairs' and substantially increased the representation of blind people on those committees with their 'distinct ring of Victorian philanthropy in their concentration on the titled, the military and the clergy'.

There's a challenge too to professional perceptions and bureaucratic solutions. When there were, in 1979, allegations that a young boy in one of America's state mental retardation institutions had been seriously abused, local politicitans tended not to believe it. It was the local self-advocacy group of people who are mentally retarded who 'phoned the boy's mother to offer support, called the press conference, launched the campaign to bolster the community alternatives to that institution. And when the local senator, primed by the institutional interest, asserted the value of the place, it was that self-advocacy group which invited him on a tour of it, the sort of tour which they, many ex-inmates, many with friends there still, knew the administrator wouldn't give him. The result? The senator changed his mind and heart and came out in favour of those community alternatives. As the group's leader says: 'He's one of the best men we've got.'

At the limit, the challenge of the new politics can seem a threat to the political order itself. A mass protest rally by Disabled in Action in New York would have ended in mass arrests if the police had not remembered in time that the city's gaols were inaccessible to wheelchairs — which was one way, at least, of bringing home the point on access that the protesters were trying to make. But official reactions can have much more serious consequences. On World Disabled Day in 1980, a peaceful demonstration in Delhi of people who were blind or had other disabilities was met on its way to deliver a petition to the Prime Minister by a lathi charge from police, and at least fifty demonstrators were reported injured.

At the limit, the challenge can seem too much of a threat to be tolerated. People with disabilities in the USSR have consistently been refused permission to set up the sort of association through which blind and deaf people have been providing workshops, training centres and social centres since the 1920s. The Action Group to Defend the Rights of the Disabled, which over the past two years has been slipping its bulletins and reports out of the country to alert the world to the deprivation of its constituents, knows how much such an association is needed. 'You should know', Yuri Kiselev, one of its leaders, has written in an open letter to fellow citizens:

> that if tragedy occurs, you will immediately find yourself in the position of an outcast, and your every move will remind you of your own helplessness . . . Nobody will protect you . . . If any of you wish to remind people of your dignity and attempt to insist on your well-declared rights — which in actuality do not exist — not only will you be persecuted, but also your parents and friends, those helping you in everyday life.[1]

The Action Group is adamant that it has nothing to do with political dissent. It simply seeks its rights under the Soviet constitution and the UN Declaration of the Rights of Disabled Persons, and it sends all its documents to the Soviet authorities in pursuit of this. The aim is not new. Kiselev, who lost both his legs in an industrial accident in 1949, has been involved in two previous attempts to set up an association, in 1956 and 1973. On both occasions, as in 1980, the official response has been that this is unnecessary, because full services are already provided. The Action Group, and the writers of the sixty or so letters of support it has been getting a month — until they dried to a trickle of only one or two in 1980 — know that there is a different perception of services from this. The Moscow Helsinki Watch Group has described in detail the deprivations of people with physical disabilities in the Soviet Union. They have no meaningful work or education; they cannot guarantee themselves a decent diet or medical attention because their pensions are too low; they have little opportunity to share in ordinary leisure pursuits; they cannot participate in sporting events, including the International Olympic Games for the Handicapped. 'These people are poor and humiliated. They are helpless, in constant need of aid, but despairing of receiving the most basic assistance. Their daily lives are a vicious cycle of alienation, loneliness and a daily struggle for survival far below the poverty level.'[2] The Action Group's bulletins build detail on this framework. According to some Western observers, it is the very specific grievances that the Action Group can document that makes it different from others concerned with more general questions of political or religious rights. It is those very specific questions that would make granting permission to form an association look like an admission that services are, after all, inadequate.

If the contrast between the position of people with physical disabilities in the USSR and the West is striking, that is not to say that the politics of disability run smoothly in Western countries. There are barriers enough to that.

The barriers may be thrown up by the organizational insensitivity of the bureaucracies which influence people's lives. The men from the English Department of Health may have been astounded and embarrassed to find that many of their fellow-participants at a seminar on the 'younger chronic sick' hospital units they were planning were potential candidates for these places. (As the man said: 'But they can't actually *leave* their homes, can they?') They may have been embarrassed and disturbed by the cogent arguments put up by these participants against what they bluntly characterized as 'prisons', and by their equally cogent arguments for supported housing. If they weren't, they should have been. But they went ahead with the plans for the units anyway, and people are living in them yet.

The barriers to the new politics may be deeply entrenched in well-established organizations. So the National Society for Mentally Handicapped Children and Adults in England, at a time of serious cuts in public expenditure in 1979, launched not an assertion of the rights of its consistuents to the services which bring equity and growth, but a 'Call for Compassion'. 'Mentally handicapped people', it said, 'cannot help themselves. We must speak for them.'

The barriers may be entrenched too in the dusty patterns of years, as one British study of consumer participation in the planning of services showed clearly enough. The organizations *for* people with disabilities were given ritual glasses of sherry four times a year by the providers of statutory services, chatted about fund-raising, exchanged information, and generally did very little in an agreeable sort of a way. The coordinating committee of organizations *of* blind people presented the providers of services with a coherent plan for action, including representation on relevant committees and demands for new resources. The committee was solid; its plan was backed by national organizations of blind people. But the providers of services thanked them, turned them down flat, and that was the end of that.

Finally, the barriers to the new politics may seem nothing but an irrelevance to many people with disabilities themselves, and the new politics an irrelevance too. There is nothing at all to say that people with disabilities will be any more or less keen than anyone else to participate in the planning, delivery and monitoring of the services they use. There is nothing to say that they will be any more or less conscious of how their society may need to be changed, or indeed that things need to be changed at all. Some activists in the United States would recognize the approach of the British Union of the Physically Impaired Against Segregation – which as a matter of policy does not reveal the size of its membership; they would share its analysis of people with disabilities as one oppressed group among others in society. Some American activists would join hands with the British Liberation Network of People with Disabilities – which doesn't tell the size of its membership either; they, like it, and like groups in the women's and other movements as well, would see 'internalized oppression' as the first barrier to be tackled. But other people with disabilities, like other women, and other blacks and other homosexuals, will find these approaches irrelevant. They might find their own version of the view of one man with multiple sclerosis: 'I feel that one should attempt to justify one's existence and that it is unfair to expect the public in general to provide special facilities for the disabled as a right. It is for the disabled themselves to accept their limitations and assist by just keeping out of the way.'

There is nothing to say, either, that people with disabilities will have any more or less of a sense of common political identity than the individuals who make up any other group which happens to share certain common characteristics. ' "The blind" as a generalized group', says one man who is totally blind himself:

can too often be very selfish, greedy and insensitive. I feel that blind people expect others both to do things for them and to make all the adjustments in a relationship, whether that be the 'relationship' of fellow pedestrians on a pavement or of a more formal or social nature. Neither do blind people seem particularly interested in allying themselves with people with other handicaps in seeking to bring about a greater degree of equity of treatment for handicapped people in general.

And even when people with disabilities do get together, the resulting in-fighting, and bickering about just how representative they are, would be recognized by many others as part of the continuing saga of political involvement. As Diane Lattin's article in *Disabled USA* was headed: 'Organizations of the Disabled: Has the Solution Become the Problem?'

Solidarity or its lack can mean different things to different people, in this political arena as any other. So one American activist talks not of Uncle Toms, but of Uncle Tiny Tims: 'It's the old "I worked my way up from the bottom, you can too. And if you're not as good as I am, of course, you don't deserve it!"'[3] To others, her anger would seem incomprehensible. They just want to get on with their lives, untrammelled by pressure to join what they see as a bunch of moaners, when they themselves have no need to moan.

So there are barriers enough to the new politics, and we don't have to know the disability arena too well to recognize them. But already, those new politics have had their effect. They have helped to create some new laws which have brought new behaviours in their wake. They have helped to create some new perceptions with which to reinforce these behaviours and from which others can be built. They have begun to create a new cycle of expectation, a cycle which spirals up instead of down. For an illustration of the way this has been happening, for a contrast between the old politics and the new, we have only to look as far as two recent pieces of legislation, one in Britain and one in the United States.

In 1970, Britain passed the Chronically Sick and Disabled Persons Act, and if it has cropped up already in these pages, that is because it covers a good many aspects of the lives of people with disabilities. For the first time, it gave local authorities the duty to provide a whole range of practical assistance to them; for the first time, there was legislation covering physical access to public buildings and much else besides. If local authorities and others had all these duties, people with disabilities could fairly claim to have corresponding rights. The Act looked like something of a breakthrough.

In fact, a decade later, it was clear that a breakthrough it wasn't. It was, indeed, a very traditional piece of British social welfare legislation, firmly based in a tradition of humane incrementalism which provides for the minority at a pace and in a way which doesn't too much disturb the majority. So it laid duties on different agencies, but provided no means at all of ensuring that they carried them out. It expressed the most humanitarian of wills, but quite understood that agencies might have other, more pressing, calls on their funds. We have already seen how the clauses on access were hedged about with the proviso that this should be ensured only when it was 'reasonable' and 'practicable' to do so, and what this has meant in practice. The approach is characteristic of the Act. So craftily is it framed that local authorities can make their own definitions of the needs that people with disabilities may have. No need, no duty — and you can't touch them for it. Certainly some people have benefited enormously under the Act — and some

American observers might well wish that they too had access to the publicly-provided aids and adaptations it offers. But others, whose needs are no different, have not benefited, and whether they have or they haven't depends very much on which part of the country they live in.

In 1973, the United States passed the Rehabilitation Act, of which Section 504 says: 'No otherwise qualified handicapped individual . . . shall, solely by reason of his or her handicap, be excluded from participation in, be denied the benefits of, or be subject to discrimination under any programme or activity receiving Federal financial assistance.' The clause doesn't apply just to employment; it covers most universities, public school systems, hospitals and nursing homes in the country; it is at the bottom of the fuss about Transbus. There is no question, in the law, of offering opportunity or acceptance only if this is 'reasonable' or 'practicable'. Citizens of the United States who have disabilities have a right to share in the common opportunities their society offers.

Section 504 and the regulations surrounding it only came into force in 1977 and then only after two massive sit-ins by people with disabilities. By the end of the decade, it was already clear enough that it was not a panacea. For a start, the American Coalition of Citizens with Disabilities was reckoning that eighty-five per cent of their constituents didn't even know their rights under this or other laws. One activist was lamenting:

> What we're finding right now is that colleges are opening up, employment is opening up — and nobody's going, nobody's jumping on those opportunities because they don't know about them, or they aren't in a position where they can accept them. And if they do try, quite often they aren't socialized enough to handle it and so they become failures, of a sort, or think they are, and they run back home.[4]

For another thing, the law applied only to Federally-supported programmes. For another again, some observers were detecting a powerful public backlash against the implications for public expenditure of making the legislation work.

By the end of the decade, too, there were intimations of the realistic limitations to any anti-discrimination legislation. In *South East College* vs. *Davis*, the first Supreme Court ruling on Section 504, the Court upheld the College against a woman with severe hearing loss who claimed that she had been illegally discriminated against because her application to train as a nurse had been refused. The Court held that 'otherwise qualified' could be taken to include essential physical attributes.

Britain knows well enough, from experience of its own anti-discrimination legislation on race and sex, that to set laws of this sort is only a preliminary to defining clearly the criteria on which they should operate. But few people would suggest that difficulties of implementation were a reason to abolish the laws. Yet it is a mark of a certain powerful strand of traditional British thinking that the large and influential Royal Association for Disability and Rehabilitation used the news of the Davis judgment to question the value of the legislation which produced it. For Britain, it urged an increase in the number of Disablement Resettlement Officers who could offer professional expertise to employers; only when there was evidence that this advice was being ignored would it be time to look to judicial solutions. 'Disabled people are a far from homogeneous group and the prejudice they face is the result of ignorance which will only be dispelled by patience and persuasion.' But others would say that persuasion has been tried for so long that patience is running out. They would say that it was time people with disabilities in Britain had a comprehensive anti-discrimination law to support them.

The approaches typified by Section 504 and the Chronically Sick and Disabled Persons Act could hardly be more different. In terms of concrete results, it is perhaps a toss-up yet which approach has achieved more for people with disabilities. But as a basis for clarity of intent, the British approach is left standing. What Section 504 asserts is what the Chronically Sick Act conspicuously doesn't, even by implication: it asserts that people with disabilities have a right to equal opportunities. It sets clear standards and norms of behaviour which are a greater force for change than ever any programme of 'public education' or persuasion. It leaves people who depart from these standards

in no doubt t[...]g in a way that society has
decided is 'a[...]e are the courts to remind
them what t[...]s a perception of people with
disabilities [...] been lost and overlaid across
the years. [...]e not objects of humanitarian
concern o[...]ffered help in a time and form
that suits[...]will of the majority, but citizens
of their c[...]ts of all others.

That[...]eaching implications. If rights are
anythir[...]divisible, not to be earned by 'con-
tributi[...]n the hope of that contribution or to
be d[...]those people who at the moment seem
'dese[...]citizens who are mentally retarded have
had [...] out what this may mean during the 1970s,
for [...] is not the only expression of the perception.
The large number of cases brought against mental retardation
institutions have asserted, and with success, that the life offered
by these places constitutes a denial of the rights which all
American citizens, whatever their IQ, are guaranteed under the
constitution. The assertion has proved a powerful impetus for
change.

If an assertion of equal rights is an assertion of the equal
consideration due to any citizen, the assertion of the right to
equal opportunity is also a starting-point for building the
services and provisions that people may need if they are to
claim those rights. Services are to be provided not in a form
that suits the providers, nor in a form that causes least incon-
venience to the majority, but in a form and in a quantity that
turns rights into realities. It is not a question of this group
getting 'too much' or that group 'too little'. It is a question
of individuals getting the specific help they need to enable
them to claim their rights, neither more nor less. Some will
need relatively little help; some will need a great deal. But no
one has any greater right to what she or he may need than
anyone else.

So we have a framework within which to build the components of services we have been looking at, for people with
disabilities no less than any others. If housing, work, education
and social security are recognized as rights in our societies,

then each service provided must be assessed in just one way: how far does it enable people to claim their rights in the context of the ordinary patterns of the society to which they belong? Equal opportunities is about adapting society to its citizens, not about expecting them to 'fit' some preconceived notion of what society 'ought' to be like.

To set the perception is one thing. To set the framework is another. To build from these the patterns of opportunity to which people have a right is the work of — how many years? But however much we stumble and slither, however much we get some things wrong and others less right than we'd hoped, at least we have a path on which to do that stumbling and slithering. At least we have a direction to hold.

14

Starting Again

When a group of children in a 'normal' school in Toronto was asked for reactions to the children with mental retardation from the 'special' class with whom they were now sharing part of their day, they said they were surprised by two things. The first was how like themselves those 'special' children were. The second was how different those children were from each other. They weren't the 'morons', the 'dafties', the 'dum-dums' any more. They were individuals, each with her or his own abilities, gifts and quirks.

Nothing that has been suggested in this book will take away the different limitations that different disabilities may bring. Medical researchers and technologists will go on looking for the 'cure' for different disabilities – and so they should. Educationalists and psychologists will continue to discover more effective ways of teaching people whose degree of mental retardation now proves too much for their skills – and so they should too. There will be advances in our understanding of our bodies and our minds, and some of these may be dramatic; there will be new technologies and some of these may bring exciting possibilities. But the Utopian dream will remain just that. What we call disability today, what we may call disability tomorrow, will not go away. And individuals will go on living with it, more or less happily, more or less despairingly, more or less angry, more or less accepting, because individuals they will continue to be.

But what the new way of looking at and providing services will do is to peel off some of the layers of handicap which have so often been imposed not just on people with disabilities but on us all. The new frameworks of service will start from a new assumption: the people we have defined as 'the disabled' will no longer find that tag a ticket to segregation from normal patterns of living the life they choose. And that will free us all, for as the boundaries of the 'norm' are widened, our social institutions will begin to express a greater tolerance of any individual difference, a greater sensitivity to any individual need.

The new patterns of politics will start from a new assumption, too: that people with disabilities are not because of this fact rendered 'incapable' of decision, objects to be pushed about at the convenience of administrators and treasurers, but that they are individuals who know as much or as little as anyone else what they want and have an equal right to the opportunity to claim it. And that too will create opportunities for us all, as we grow in our understanding of how our societies' structures can be modified to encourage cooperation and equity.

The overturning of the old assumptions will not be easy. It will bring risk and challenge. 'The easy way out is always to say, "Yes, we must impose more controls because we are bothered about people dying," ' says Selwyn Goldsmith in his *Designing for the Disabled.* 'The more difficult alternative is to say, "No, we shall not, because we are concerned about people living." ' He was writing about fire regulations, but his words could apply to many other areas than that.

It is perhaps because of the risk and challenge that we prefer instead to spend a great deal more time talking about 'changing attitudes' than we do daring to change laws and with them expectations of behaviour. We talk about 'public education' and patience, and 'moving at a pace the community can accept'. But none of us, whether we are defined as mentally retarded or not, is much good at working to a hypothesis; our inclination will always be to settle for what we have. We don't have to look very deeply at the history of social reform to recognize that changes in 'public' attitudes don't create changes in provision and norms of behaviour, but follow them. And we don't have to look very deeply into that history either to recognize that in daring to change we are not simply making some humanitarian gesture for a group called 'them', or even recog-

190

nising 'their' rights. What we are doing, we are doing for the health and growth of us all, both as individuals and as that collection of individuals and groups which is called society. When we start to peel off some of the layers of handicap that we have imposed on disability, and some of the layers of mutual handicap that we have imposed on that, we are beginning to free not just those people we define as 'disabled', but the 'able' others as well. If the handicap is mutual, so is the growth, and it is in mutual exploration of the first that we shall all be on the way to the second.

'We face more obviously than more', said Paul Hunt of people with severe disabilities in 'A Critical Condition':

the universal problem of coming to terms with the fact of man's individuality and loneliness. If we begin to accept our own special pecularity, we shall be in a position to help others to accept even their own difference from everyone else. These two acceptances are bound up together. People's shocked reactions to the obvious deviant often reflect their own deepest fears and difficulties, their failure to accept themselves as they really are, and the other person simply as 'other'. The disabled person's 'strangeness' can manifest and symbolize all differences between human beings. In his relations with more nearly normal people, he may become a medium for reconciling them to the fact of these differences, and demonstrate their relative unimportance compared to what we have in common.

People with disabilities are not 'normal'. However our definitions of what is normal change with time, people whose disabilities are severe enough to demand that society adapts to encompass them will remain 'abnormal', in the statistical sense at least. But if that abnormality were not something to be shunned, if it demanded instead only adaptation of common social patterns, the gains would be enormous. We would all have taken some steps to free ourselves from the tyranny that the 'norm' can impose. We would all be that much freer to stop looking over our shoulders at the behaviour of others for guidance on our own. We would all be on the way to under-

191

standing that it is normal to be different. The children in the Toronto school were beginning to learn the lesson. Children in Britain who have the good fortune to pick up books like *How We Play* will begin to learn very young that 'we' includes people with spectacles, funny thin legs, children who are black, children who are white, children who go about in wheelchairs. They will even learn that we can get pretty angry with each other sometimes, whether we are in a wheelchair or not. Are we then to put limits on the growth of children by segregating them from each other and teaching them, in their separate groups, that it is 'normal' to be apart?

'We can witness to the truth', said Paul Hunt again:

> that a person's dignity does not rest even in his consciousness, and certainly that it does not rest in his beauty, age, intelligence or colour. Those of us with unimpaired minds but severely disabled bodies, have a unique opportunity to show other people not only that our big difference from them does not lessen our worth, but also that *no* difference between men, however real, unpleasant and disturbing, does away with their right to be treated as fully human.

And what he says about people whose disabilities are physical applies every bit as much to people who are mentally retarded. When we accept that every person has the same rights, that rights are indivisible and not to be somehow 'earned' by competence, we shall perhaps be on the way to holding this shaky world together with rather more secure notions than the ones we have operated by in the past.

We might learn, for a start, something about the limitations of notions of 'independence' in a world where individuals find themselves increasingly divided one from another, and where gulfs between nations are bridged by the flimsiest of economic tightropes. We might start to recognize out loud that dependence is in itself a value, essential in many of our personal and collective dealings; that independence is a pretty slim hope on which to build our security for the future; that interdependence is the sort of goal that makes sense. We have seen how past policies towards people with disabilities have set 'independence' as the goal. We have seen something of the hurdles that some people with disabilities negotiate to reach it. We have seen enough of the penalties imposed on those who stumble and of the segregation of the back ward. But we have seen something, too, of the way out of this tyranny. We can glimpse the way forward from the people with severe disabilities who say that the goal for them is not to spend hours and energy in coping alone with the essentials of everyday life, but to be able to choose whether they do this by themselves or with help from another. Some will choose one way, some another and there is nothing at all to say that individual preference is 'right' or 'wrong' either way. If that choice became real for people with disabilities, it would become no less important for us all. We could then all be on the way to a recognition of interdependence that carries no blame, of weakness, that carries no shame.

And we could be on the way, too, to a recognition that the 'contribution' that people make to their society is not simply to be defined in narrow economic terms, that those who are out of the job market are not somehow less for that, that everyone has a share of gifts and talents as well as capacities to irritate and alienate, and that all of them are needed to make up the whole. The recognition doesn't at all imply that people with disabilities should carry the job of spear-heading us to some post-industrial age; they have the right to be as unemployed as the rest of us, not twice as unemployed or more. But it is still a recognition that we all need, wherever the vagaries of Western economics take us next.

Finally, an end to the segregation of people with disabilities from the opportunity to share in the ordinary patterns and expectations of life will bring us all, whether we number ourselves among them or not, closer to what may look like a paradox. We may find that we need the impaired to make us whole – and that both individually and collectively.

We have seen enough of the perceptions of uncleanness, evil, tragedy and even un-humanness with which people with disabilities have been lumbered, and enough of the practices which have flowed from these perceptions, to recognize that there is a very strong tendency in us all – and again whether we are classed as disabled or not — to put as much distance as possible between the clean, good, healthy and happy selves we would like to be and the reminder that we are not altogether any of these things. We have seen enough to recognize that the working out of these perceptions in the small world of the residential institution is no more than a dramatic and intensified version of its working out in the larger world in which we all live.

To end the segregation will not abolish either the perceptions or the practices overnight. They run too deep for that. But what it could do is enable us all to see more clearly what we were trying to put away. And then we may choose instead to start to meet it, to begin to recognize in ourselves what we were trying to avoid by dumping it on the people we have defined as less 'normal' than we are. And that is the beginning of growth towards individual and collective wholeness.

Notes

1 Starting Points

1 Where the titles of published works are not in the text, they can be found in the Bibliography at the end of the book.
2 Quotations throughout the book are from personal communications, unless otherwise identified; some have been previously recorded in *Listen* (1973) and *Our Life* (1972), both by Ann Shearer and published by the Campaign for the Mentally Handicapped.
3 From Audette, R., 'Listen! Let us Speak', in *New Neighbors,* President's Committee on Mental Retardation, Washington DC 1974.

2 Whose Problem?

1 Both quotations from Silver Jubilee Committee on Improving Access for Disabled People, *Can Disabled People Go Where You Go?* DHSS, London 1979.

3 Family Matters

1 Both quotations from Harris, A., *Handicapped and Impaired in Great Britain*, HMSO, London 1971.
2 From Craft, A. and M., *Handicapped Married Couples,* Routledge & Kegan Paul, London 1980.
3 From Baldwin, S., *Sometimes it seems as if you're left to cope all on your own,* Department of Social Administration and Social Work, University of York 1978.
4 Ibid.
5 From 'Who Cares about the Carers?', *Spinal Injuries Association Newsletter,* no. 13, July 1979.

4 Making Contact

1 From Connolly, R., 'A w-w-word in y-your ear . . . ', *Observer* colour magazine, 20 July 1980.

2   From Mimmack, J., 'Physical Relationships and the Disabled Woman', *Spare Rib,* September 1979.
3   Ibid.

6   *Perceptions and Practices*

1   From Shearer, A., *A Community Service for Mentally Handicapped Children,* Barnardo's, London 1978.
2   From Audette, R., 'Listen! Let us Speak', in *New Neighbors,* President's Committee on Mental Retardation, Washington DC 1974.

7   *Institutions and their Inhabitants*

1   From Audette, R., 'Listen! Let us Speak', in *New Neighbors,* President's Committee on Mental Retardation, Washington DC 1974.
2   From Hunt, P., 'Comment: Single Rooms', *Cheshire Smile,* Winter 1968–69.
3   From Mattinson, J., *Marriage and Mental Handicap,* Duckworth, London 1970.

8   *The Cycle of Expectation*

1   From Shearer, A., *Community Service for Mentally Handicapped Children*, Barnardo's, London 1978.
2   From Tomalin, C., 'Why must my son have to suffer this extra handicap?', *The Times,* 12 June 1980.
3   From Audette, R., 'Listen! Let us Speak', in *New Neighbors,* President's Committee on Mental Retardation, Washington DC 1974.
4   From Loach, I. and Lister, R., *Second Class Disabled,* Equal Rights for Disabled Women Campaign, London 1978.
5   From ' "Free the People": Interview with Cass Irwin', *Disabled USA*, vol. 3, no. 5, 1980.

9   *Housing*

1   From Brett, B., *Housing for the Disabled,* unpublished paper, Colchester 1980.

10   *Education*

1   From Beresford, P. and Tuckwell, P., *Schools for All,* MIND/ Campaign for the Mentally Handicapped, London 1978.
2   The figures refer, as do the Government's proposals on the reform of special education, to England and Wales. Scotland has its own educational system.
3   Quoted in Anderson, E. and Spain, B., *The Child with Spina Bifida,* Methuen, London 1977.

11 Work

1 All these quotations from Sainsbury, S., *Registered as Disabled*, Bell, London 1970.
2 From Scourse, P., 'The Life Sentence of Unemployment', *Sunday Times*, 16 July 1978.
3 From Sainsbury, S., *Registered as Disabled*, Bell, London 1970.
4 From Scourse, P., 'The Life Sentence of Unemployment', *Sunday Times*, 16 July 1978.
5 From Tyne, A., *Working Out*, Campaign for the Mentally Handicapped, London 1975.

13 Politics

1 From 'Disability in the USSR', *Rehabilitation World*, New York, Summer/Autumn 1979.
2 Ibid.
3 From ' "Free the People": Interview with Cass Irwin', *Disabled USA*, vol 3, no. 5, 1980.
4 Ibid.

Bibliography

The books and essays cited here don't include all those I have consulted, but simply those on which I have drawn most heavily or which are referred to in the text. Where a work is referred to in more than one chapter, it is listed under each.

1 Starting Points

Harris, A., *Handicapped and Impaired in Great Britain*, HMSO, London 1971
Townsend, P., *Poverty in the United Kingdom*, Penguin, Harmondsworth 1979

2 Whose Problem?

Ashley, J., *Journey into Silence*, Bodley Head, London 1973
Hewitt, S., *The Family and the Handicapped Child*, George Allen & Unwin, London 1970
Hunt, P., 'A Critical Condition', in Hunt, P., ed. *Stigma*, Geoffrey Chapman, London 1966
Kew, S., *Handicap and Family Crisis*, Pitman, London 1975
Mussett, H., *The Untrodden Ways*, Gollancz, London 1975
Schaefer, N., *Does She Know She's There?* Futura, London 1979
Thomas, D., *The Social Psychology of Childhood Disability*, Methuen, London 1978
Wright, B., *Physical Disability, a Psychological Approach*, Harper and Row, New York 1960

'Some Psycho-Social Aspects of Disability', in Malikin, D. and Rusalem, H., *The Vocational Rehabilitation of the Disabled*, University of London Press, London 1969

3 Family Matters

President's Committee on Mental Retardation, *Mental Retardation – the Leading Edge: Service Programmes that Work*, Washington DC 1978

Sutton, A. H., 'Marriage and the Handicapped', in Lancaster Gaye, D., ed. *Personal Relationships, the Handicapped and the Community*, Routledge & Kegan Paul, London 1972

4 Making Contact

Sutton, A. H., 'Marriage and the Handicapped', in Lancaster Gaye, D., ed. *Personal Relationships, the Handicapped and the Community*, Routledge & Kegan Paul, London 1972

Thunem, J., 'The Invalid Mind', in Hunt, P., ed. *Stigma*, Geoffrey Chapman, London 1966

Williams, P., *Our Mutual Handicap*, Campaign for the Mentally Handicapped, London 1979

5 Getting Together

Hayle, G., *The Source Book for the Disabled*, Paddington Press, London 1979

Shepard, A., 'One Body', in Hunt, P., ed. *Stigma*, Geoffrey Chapman, London 1966

Silver Jubilee Committee on Improving Access for Disabled People, *Can Disabled People Go Where You Go?* DHSS, London 1979

6 Perceptions and Practices

Brown, R., *Find Debbie*, Peacock Books, Harmondsworth 1979

Burnett, F. H., *The Secret Garden*, Puffin Books, Harmondsworth 1968

Burt, C., *The Young Delinquent*, University of London, London 1925

Craig, M., *Blessings*, Hodder, London 1979

Finkelstein, V., *Attitudes and Disabled People: Issues for Discussion*, World Rehabilitation Fund, New York 1980

Goffman, E., *Stigma*, Pelican Books, Harmondsworth 1968

Hasler, E., *Martin is Our Friend*, Methuen, London 1979

Hibbert, C., *The Roots of Evil*, Penguin, Harmondsworth 1966

Hunt, P., 'A Critical Condition', in Hunt, P., ed. *Stigma*, Geoffrey Chapman, London 1966

Millar, E. and Gwynne, G., *A Life Apart*, Tavistock Publications, London 1972

Opie, P. and I., *The Lore and Language of Schoolchildren*, OUP, Oxford 1959
  The Oxford Dictionary of Nursery Rhymes, Clarendon Press, Oxford 1951

Oswin, M., *Children Living in Long Stay Hospitals*, Spastics International Medical Publications, Heinemann Medical, London 1978

Rook, D., *Run Wild, Run Free*, Scholastic Books Services, 1969

Thunem, J., 'The Invalid Mind', in Hunt, P., ed. *Stigma*, Geoffrey Chapman, London 1966

Wolfensberger, W., *The Origins and Nature of our Institutional Models*, University of Syracuse, Syracuse 1974

7 Institutions and their Inhabitants

Battye, L., 'The Chatterley Syndrome', in Hunt, P., ed. *Stigma*, Geoffrey Chapman, London 1966

Hunt, P., 'A Critical Condition', in Hunt P., ed. *Stigma*, Geoffrey Chapman, London 1966

Millar, E. and Gwynne, G., *A Life Apart*, Tavistock Publications, London 1972

Oswin, M., *Children Living in Long Stay Hospitals*, Spastics International Medical Publications, Heinemann Medical, London 1978

Scull, A., *Decarceration*, Prentice-Hall, New Jersey 1977

8 *The Cycle of Expectation*

Archives of Physical Medicine and Rehabilitation, Vol. 60, No. 10, 1979

Fallon, B., *So You're Paralysed*, Spinal Injuries Association, London 1975

Guggenbuhl Craig, A., *Power in the Helping Professions*, Spring Publications, Zurich 1976

Scott, R., 'The Construction of Concepts of Stigma by Professional Experts', in Boswell, D., and Wingrove, J., eds. *The Handicapped Person in the Community*, Tavistock Publications, London 1974

Whelan, E., and Speake, B., *Adult Training Centres in England and Wales*, National Association of Teachers of the Mentally Handicapped, London 1977

9 *Housing*

Buckle, J., *Work and Housing of Impaired Persons in Great Britain*, HMSO, London 1971

Goldsmith, S., *Designing for the Disabled*, Royal Institute of British Architects, London 1976

King's Fund Centre, *An Ordinary Life*, King's Fund Centre, London 1980

Report of the Committee of Enquiry into Mental Handicap Nursing and Care, Cmnd. 7468, HMSO, London 1979

Thomas, D., Firth, H. and Kendall, A., *ENCOR — A Way Ahead*, Campaign for the Mentally Handicapped, London 1978

10 Education

Anderson, E., *Making Ordinary Schools Special*, College of Special Education, London 1971

Anderson, E. and Cope, C., *Special Units in Ordinary Schools*, University of London Institute of Education, London 1977

Committee of Enquiry into the Education of Handicapped Children and Young People, *Special Educational Needs*, Cmnd. 7212, HMSO, London 1978

Department of Education and Science, *Behavioural Units*, London 1978

11 Work

Jordan, D., *A New Employment Programme wanted for Disabled People*, Disability Alliance, London 1979

Kettle, M., *Disabled People and their Employment*, Association of Disabled Professionals, London 1979

Townsend, P., *Poverty in the United Kingdom*, Penguin, Harmondsworth 1979

12 Economics

Disability Alliance, *Disability Rights Handbook*, Disability Alliance, London 1980

Hale, G., ed. *Sourcebook for the Disabled*, Paddington Press, London 1979

Hunt, P., 'A Critical Condition', in Hunt, P., ed. *Stigma*, Geoffrey Chapman, London 1966

Topliss, E., *Provision for the Disabled*, Blackwell, Oxford 1979

Townsend, P., *Poverty in the United Kingdom*, Penguin, Harmondsworth 1979

13 Politics

'Disability in the USSR', *Rehabilitation World*, Rehabilitation International, New York, Summer/Autumn 1979

Lattin, D., 'Organizations of the Disabled: Has the Solution become the Problem?', in *Disabled USA*, Vol. 2 No. 10, President's Committee on Employment of the Handicapped, Washington 1979

Low, C., Rose, G. and Cranshaw, B., *Participation in Services for the Handicapped: Two Contrasting Models*, Personal Social Services Council, London 1979

14 Starting Again

Goldsmith, S., *Designing for the Disabled*, Royal Institute of British Architects, London 1976

Harper, A. and Roche, C., *How We Play*, Kestrel Books, London 1979

Hunt, P., 'A Critical Condition', in Hunt, P., ed. *Stigma*, Geoffrey Chapman, London 1966

Index

205